ONE INCREASING PURPOSE

MALDWYN L. EDWARDS

ONE
INCREASING PURPOSE

BY

MALDWYN EDWARDS
M.A. (Wales), M.A. (Cantab.), Ph.D. (London)

The Social Service Lecture, 1947

Yet I doubt not thro' the ages one increasing purpose runs,
And the thoughts of men are widen'd with the process of the suns.
(TENNYSON: 'Locksley Hall')

THE EPWORTH PRESS
(EDGAR C. BARTON)
25–35 CITY ROAD, LONDON, E.C.1

*Published for the Social
Service Lecture Trust*

Made in Great Britain

TO

PETER

FROM HIS UNCLE

PREFACE

IT IS AN honour to be invited to follow in the distinguished succession of those who have been invited to deliver the Beckly Lecture. There were many tempting lines of thought to follow in the choice of a subject. My beloved friend, the late Rev. S. E. Keeble, suggested fourteen possible subjects and all seemed promising, even though so many were not within my true competence. The line I have taken might seem at least semi-theological, but I can at least plead that it has been for a long time on my heart and mind. So often in meetings there are references to the Kingdom of God in politics, or in industry or in society. The phrase is undoubtedly associated in people's minds with material and moral betterment, but no clear meaning seems to be attached to the social reference. This Lecture is a contribution toward an understanding of the part God expects us to play in the realization of His own increasing purpose.

I wish to acknowledge my deep indebtedness to Dr. W. F. Lofthouse, who has read through the manuscript and made most valuable suggestions. I am also glad to acknowledge a long-standing debt of gratitude to my close friend, Mr. Crofton Gane. He has read through the pages concerned with industry and made his own wise comments.

Finally, I want again to say how much I owe to Miss Gwenda Smith, who has typed the book with such painstaking care.

I am indeed grateful to the following authors and publishers who have kindly given me permission to quote from their copyright works.

Messrs. Macmillan and Co. Ltd.

and Mrs. George Bambridge for a few lines from 'We and They', *Debits and Credits*, by Rudyard Kipling; for lines from *The Dynasts*, by Thomas Hardy; and for an extract from *Does God Exist?*, by Professor A. E. Taylor.

Messrs. Allen and Unwin Ltd.

For an extract from *History is on Our Side*, by Dr. Joseph Needham.

Edward Arnold and Co.

For an extract from *History of Europe*, by H. A. L. Fisher.

Constable and Co. Ltd.

and Mr. Bernard Shaw for an extract from *The Irrational Knot*.

MALDWYN EDWARDS.

CONTENTS

ANALYSIS OF THE ARGUMENT

AMONG THE many misadventures of Jerome K. Jerome's three men in a boat was the heartbreaking task of threading their way through a maze. They found themselves continually doubling back upon their tracks until their patience was exhausted. There was, of course, a way to the centre, and a guide could have led them through at once. It would be enough to cause misgivings in anyone's mind if this book was likened to a maze. There is, however, one sustained argument running through the separate chapters, and it might avoid any perplexities if I set out in simple terms what is the clue to the whole.

In an age in which there is a decay of belief, the agnostic may refuse to follow the comfortless logic of his creed and strive instead to find a plan where none (on his premises) can exist. It is only belief in God that gives us a plan for living, for then we know that life came not by chance but design. In a law-abiding universe we can properly look for those laws which govern our inner lives. In this way we can see the clues which God has given us for an understanding of His world. But the supreme reason why the Christian knows that history has a meaning is because God has shown His plan for the world in the teaching of Jesus as it is lit up and interpreted by His life and death and rising again.

This plan can be understood within the framework of our Lord's teaching about the Kingdom of God. In a real sense the Kingdom is present. The King is already on His throne and His laws are already in operation. Even now there is the victory over sin and death, and at any instant a man may make the Kingdom his own possession. It is also true that in the end God alone can consummate His Kingdom and put the last enemy under His feet. But the Kingdom not only stands; it grows. As more and more come into the Kingdom, so more and more the Kingdom grows. It is the reign of God in men's hearts and in order that the creatures may own that sway, there are three tasks to be accomplished. They cannot be separated in time for all three proceed together, and all are necessary. There is first of all the task of demolition. All those social habits which have evil consequences must be attacked because they hinder the

King from entering into His own. Reformers who attack private and social vice do God's work.

The second task is creating those right conditions of life whereby men can more easily recognize the King in His beauty and bow the knee to Him. This work is to be done in the world of politics, of society, and of business. If in developing the argument in these three spheres my eyes have been upon this country in particular, the same argument must be extended to the life of man in every land. God intends men to enjoy the good life in its fullness, and that necessitates a worthy setting.

But these two tasks do only provide the setting, for the good life is not to be assessed in material terms. It consists in the response of the soul to God. It is the reign of a God within the believer's heart. This brings us to the third great task which is the proclamation of the Word. God has entrusted this Gospel of invitation to the Church alone, and He has fashioned the instrument for the performance of the task. In God's eyes the Church is not many but one, and the Holy Spirit is leading the Church into an acceptance of that truth. As yet there is nothing to indicate that there will be uniformity of organization, but we are being led into a unity of spirit.

The one Church can by its very witness bring men to a solution of the three greatest modern problems. It can by its teaching and witness make lasting peace in the world; an economic prosperity shared by all, and freedom for the individual man.

This is not, however, the only work which the Church in its united witness can accomplish. Its main task is evangelical, for in the Christian Faith there is the one deliverance from the contradictions of our human nature. Despite education, science, political machinery, and economics, we have watched in our century man's best endeavours ending in two world wars with their long and tragic aftermath. There has been ample evidence that nothing within our civilization can save us, for nothing can reach down to the black depths of the human heart. Our deliverance is of God, and it is this message which the Church exists to proclaim.

Inside the Church as well as outside there are those who cast down and those who build up that a highway may be prepared for our God. But though all must serve these two ends of God through their particular work, Christians unite in the third task of witnessing to man's need of God and God's availability for man. So God makes use of many workmen for his *one increasing purpose* to reign in every heart alone. Some are blind instruments, and the invitation to come into the Church is in essence the invitation to become the conscious instruments of God and to share in that travail by which His Kingdom comes.

The great message for our age is that within the one fellowship of all believers men should follow their own vocations informed by a common purpose, and that through their faithfulness, joy should be in widest commonalty spread. Then can we be bold to say: Thy Kingdom come.

CHAPTER ONE

THE ONE PLAN

CHARLES DARWIN was the most amiable of men, and it is ironic that so great a controversy broke over that unoffending head. For when he propounded his theory of evolution the long alliance between religion and science came abruptly to an end. C. E. Raven has shown how deep and fruitful was that alliance, and he has spoken of the conflict over Darwin's views as the 'storm in a Victorian tea-cup'.[a] Doubtless there was no need for such wordy warfare. For long years the substance of his theory has been welcomed by Christians because it throws a new and revealing light on God's method in creation, and heightens the wonder of the natural world. But to his contemporaries the storm could be contained in no tea-cup. It blackened the face of the earth. It is true that this fresh approach to biology destroyed any literal acceptance of the Genesis story, any idea of absolute creation—but to very many this meant a denial of Christian truth. Take away the six days in which God worked, and you take away God. Bishop Wilberforce may have been soundly trounced by Huxley, but he spoke for great numbers of the faithful. What indeed was happening to a tidy, ordered Universe? There was not only the attack from without, but the attack of the higher critics from within. How dangerous the harmless Bishop Colenso seemed. There were heresy hunts in Anglicanism, Presbyterianism, and Methodism. They came because Christians were on the defensive and protested the more vehemently, because they felt the less secure. Tennyson, the most representative poet of the age, reflects the confidence that was subject to odd and unsuspected pangs of misgiving. Swinburne was the good pagan whose evidence can on this issue be discounted. Robert Browning was ready to declare

> *The best is yet to be,*
> *The last of life, for which the first was made.*[b]

He could say in his unshaken faith:

> *This world's no blot for us,*
> *Nor blank; it means intensely, and means good:*
> *To find its meaning is my meat and drink.*[c]

[a] *Science, Religion, and the Future* (1943). [b] *Rabbi ben Ezra.* [c] *Fra Lippo Lippi.*

But Tennyson was not quite so sure:

> *Oh yet we trust that somehow good*
> *Will be the final goal of ill.*[a]

He was persuaded that there lived 'more faith in honest doubt' than in half the creeds.

By the end of the century that doubt had in the minds of many crystallized into unbelief. The corrosive acids of criticism had burnt away their faith. The old authority of religion had dissolved, and they stood like children who suddenly discover they are lost, and stare with frightened face at an unfamiliar universe. But once God has gone, what significance has history? Kierkegaard, Dostoevski, and Nietzsche have been read with such absorbing zeal in this century because they speak of what men know. They have wrestled with the demons of doubt, and fear, and remained to tell their story. The first two had their dark night of the soul, but out of agony re-discovered God. Nietzsche had no such deliverance. God was dead, but the flippant need not feel easy. If there is no God, there is not cosmos, but chaos. The only order in the world is the one that man imposes on it. Since man was left to his own resources, there was need for the old heroic barbarian virtues. The world was not for weaklings, but for supermen.

In our own country the decay of belief in God has resulted in two schools of thought. A novelist, a poet, and a philosopher may speak for the grimmer philosophy. Thomas Hardy could speak of 'a local cult called Christianity'[b] because God was a figment of men's minds, and Christ a Jewish teacher, nothing more. The sombre brooding melancholy of the 'great inviolate' Egdon waste, indifferent in its 'ancient permanence' to the changing rivers, fields, and men, is a symbol of the vast indifferent universe in which man had perforce to play his part. Tess is a puppet in the hands of the President of the Immortals, and who is he but 'an Aeschylean phrase'? Life had no meaning and therefore no direction.

> *Like a knitter drowsed,*
> *Whose fingers play in skilled unmindfulness,*
> *The Will has woven with an absent heed*
> *Since life first was; and ever so will weave.*[c]

[a] *In Memoriam.*   [b] *The Dynasts*, I. vi.   [c] ibid.

William Ernest Henley is not remembered as a great poet but as one who in his life, as well as his poetry, expressed the spirit of the stoic, caught in the fell clutch of circumstance. When he cried out that he was the master of his fate, the captain of his soul, it was a superb piece of braggadocio. He did not stand in insolent and arrogant defiance. It was simply that he knew no God to whom one bends the knee.

> *A poor old tramp explains his poor old ulcers.*
> *Life is (I think) a blunder and a shame.*[a]

No philosopher has expressed this point of view more uncompromisingly than Bertrand Russell. Thermodynamics speaks the doom of life. It is as certain as anything may be certain that nothing lies beyond us. All therefore that is left for us is to stand on the 'hard rock of unyielding despair'. It may not be a comforting reflection, but it is the brave statement of a man who refuses to pretend there is comfort where none can be found.

But this is not the only view of a universe in which the throne is empty. The scientific humanists have achieved the startling feat of rejecting God whilst still accepting the unity and intelligibility of the universe. They can ask men to be obedient to spiritual values even though these values have no objective validity and are only the product of social custom and behaviour; the pooled thinking of man concerning the highest standards man can know. They take a highly popular line when they want the fruits of religion without the tree itself. It is in fact what Julian Huxley calls 'religion without revelation'. Popular scientific writers like J. D. Bernal, C. H. Waddington, and Lancelot Hogben have helped to clarify the distinctive tenets of this new faith. Man, like any spider, can from himself spin out his own values. The wayfaring man might, in his folly, have thought that, since such values are not grounded in an eternal order, they partake the nature of man-made temporal things. But this is not so. For these scientists, turned philosophers, are able to give them not a relative but an absolute significance. Having done that, it is no great difficulty to show that man can achieve his destiny if he will be reasonable, and adopt a scientific attitude. If we will leave the dark shadows, we can climb to our high estate.

This means that like the French astronomer Laplace they

a *In Hospital.*

B

'have no need of the hypothesis of God', but yet can find a meaning in history. It is a philosophical judgement which has a long ancestry. Henri Bergson's *élan vital* is the *anima mundi* of the ancients decked out in modern dress. And this again has close affinity with the blind struggling god of the earlier H. G. Wells, thrusting life forward, though all unknowing. Bernard Shaw pursues this same idea in his conception of the immanental force whose unconscious ends are served by us. 'Though the Life Force supplies us with its own purpose, it has no other brains to work with than those it has painfully and imperfectly evolved in our heads.'[a] The dialogue in Hell between Don Juan and the Devil, with Ana and the Statue as heated disputants, making their occasional interpositions, is a long conversation on the Life Force and its work. The Devil, very wisely on his premises, concludes the universe has no purpose, but Don Juan will have no such pessimism. The Life Force which has done wonderful things unconsciously by taking a line of least resistance, wants to know its way and destination, and so it takes a philosopher's brain to grasp knowledge for its use. In the service of that Life Force Don Juan is willing to be employed.[b]

The scientific humanists may use their own idiom, but this is fundamentally their point of view. The universe intends man to get on. It does not provide an escalator, but if man will use reason and effort, the force of Life will be at his back in his laborious ascent. Many scientists are Marxian in outlook, and their political views lend added weight to their cheerful belief of design in history. In a book recently published, Dr. Joseph Needham chose the illuminating title: *History is on Our Side*. In an earlier book, *The Sceptical Biologist*, Dr. Needham had stated categorically that the 'concept of Revelation has been removed from science'. In this book he gladly accepts that Marxian analysis which explains history in terms of dialectical materialism. He has no difficulty in accepting an analogy between evolution in the world of nations and the world of man. He even dares to say that 'sociological development is continuous with biological'. After the class struggle which has assumed different forms in different epochs, there will be the dictatorship of the proletariat, and that will lead to the classless state. He has no God, but he can ascribe the powers of God to a mysterious 'it', and conclude with the saintly Julian of Norwich that 'all shall be well'. 'That

[a] Preface to *The Irrational Knot*, p. 25 (1905). [b] *Man and Superman*, Act 3.

great force, if so we may consider it, which has brought about
the evolutionary development of our earth, and of the life upon
it, is beyond reasonable doubt still at work, and in this sense
collectivism is inevitable. Life is essentially order and organization; man in his societies cannot be untrue to it. History is on
his side.'[a] That statement may sound incredibly naïve, but
J. B. S. Haldane, J. D. Bernal, and all their school, would not
dispute a word of it.

It was understandable in Herbert Spencer to whom evolution
was a holy word and applicable in its workings to the whole of
life. He could declare in his *Social Statics* that progress is not an
accident, but a necessity; a part of nature. But he did not live
to see two world wars shatter men's complacency. It was likewise understandable in Marx who, receiving his dialectics from
Hegel and his materialism from Feuerbach, was able with Hegel
to read a meaning into history even though his unifying thread
was so vastly different. His philosophy was illogical, but his life
was lived within the nineteenth century of evolutionary optimism.
The storm clouds had not broken.

It is no reflection on a well-known chain of shops to say that
this 'Marx and Spencer' philosophy has been cheapened by
events. But still they stand in serried ranks—the scientific thinkers
who, discounting God, can still read purpose into history. Where
lies the truth in this tussle between agnostic pessimists and agnostic
optimists? And in particular, which has the proper philosophy
of history consistent with a disbelief in God? It is strange to
accept design where there is no Designer, and to believe in
purpose where there is no Mind. The humanist and the Marxist
can speak of the world as law-abiding and yet believe it is 'a for-
tuitous concourse of atoms'. Unbelief in such circumstances
imposes a greater strain on credulity than belief could ever do.
H. A. L. Fisher was surely far more true to his agnosticism when
he asserted in his Preface to the *History of Europe* that one intel-
lectual excitement had been denied him. 'Men wiser and more
learned than I have discovered in history a plot, a rhythm,
a predetermined pattern. These harmonies are concealed from
me. I can see only one emergency following up another as wave
follows wave, only one great fact with respect to which, since it
is unique, there can be no generalizations, only one safe rule for
the historian: that he should recognize in the development of

[a] Dr. Joseph Needham, *History is on Our Side*, p. 27 (1946).

human destinies the play of the contingent and the unforeseen.' This seems to me a forthright and altogether consistent consequence of his philosophy.

Thomas Hardy and Bertrand Russell are right. If we have been cast blindly on the shores of time we shall likewise be swept blindly into the dusty, unremembering grave. If there is no God, neither will there be a pattern set in the heavens. The only meaning the world can have is a meaning we impose on it. It has no rhyme nor reason of its own. George R. Sims in one of his novels depicted a world which, owing to the deep-laid plot of two men, fell victim to the delusion that the resurrection had not taken place. Christianity was discredited, and with it came a collapse of belief in God. Some few held to their former ideals, because, God or no God, they offered a better way of life. But the vast majority abandoned themselves to unrestrained indulgence. Let us eat, drink, and be merry, they argued, for tomorrow we die. No one would wish to preserve belief in God only because it affords sanctions for right conduct. But it is certain that the ordinary man in his common sense, would not accept the humanism of the cultivated. If there is no God then the race goes to the swift, the battle goes to the strong, and the weakest go to the wall.

Bolingbroke in a well-quoted phrase wrote about 'the dignity of history'. But one can only speak thus when man has a dignified part to play in a plan determined by God. Shakespeare showed profound insight when he pictured Macbeth losing his sense of history when he lost his sense of God. After he had exchanged Providence for Witches, no way could be traced through the darkling mists.

> *And all our yesterdays have lighted fools*
> *The way to dusty death.*

Life became

> *a tale*
> *Told by an idiot, full of sound and fury,*
> *Signifying nothing.*[a]

It is only belief in God that can make history luminous. When the gardener has straightened his back, given a last loving scrutiny at his garden, put on his coat and gone down the garden path, when the physicist and chemist have finished their work in the

a *Macbeth*, v, 16.

laboratories, and the astronomer has left his giant telescope, it would be for the good of all if their paths converged and they could talk together. Suppose for one mad moment there could be a pooling of the wonder and interest scientific workers feel in their respective spheres, and suppose to that exciting brew, could be added 'the poets' dream', would not that heady mixture intoxicate us with the marvel of creation when the morning stars sang together, and all the sons of God shouted for joy?

Or more prosaically, if it was possible to secure not a pooling of wonder but just a pooling of information; supposing that all the laws men discover in their separate branches of knowledge could be correlated to give us an integrated picture of the world, would we not marvel at the evidence of an all-embracing design? Such a conspectus we do not know. We know of the scientist turned theologian, or more rarely the theologian turned scientist. Sometimes, as in the case of Leonardo da Vinci, one man in his time will play many parts. But he is sufficiently rare for others to point admiringly at him. How many branches of science are there? Add to them all the knowledge of artist, musician and poet, philosopher, psychologist, and medical doctor. Supplement with the knowledge of craftsmen in their various media, and swell the data with the evidence men can bring from other walks of life. The rustics gazed at Goldsmith's village parson, and as they gazed the wonder grew 'that one small head could carry all he knew'. But there is no head that could carry the accumulated wisdom of men. Still less can such knowledge be rightly fitted together for men to see the world as it really is.[a] That synthesis demands the mind of God. He remains His own interpreter. His judgements are unsearchable and his ways past finding. But we can realize dimly both the order and the magic of all created things.

Paley's putting of the argument from design may seem out of date, but the argument itself is unaffected. The great philosopher, A. E. Taylor, restated the argument and in particular drew attention to a notable fact. Numerous insects will make an adaptation to a remote future, so that the advantage is secured to the benefit of the still unborn offspring and not the egg-depositing insect.[b] Organic nature is pervaded with this forward-looking adaptation,

---

[a] 'It is notorious that preoccupation with one kind of evidence may actually impair a man's power of dealing with evidence of a different kind.' A. E. Taylor, *Does God Exist?*, p. 40.
[b] ibid., p. 48.

and a mechanistic explanation is clearly inadequate. He argues that the appearance and persistence of intelligent and purposeful species of organisms mean that a directing and controlling intelligence has been at work on the formation of the environment by which alone they live. Thus design is woven into the whole fabric of nature. His conclusion is strongly stated. 'It seems to me (and I know that better philosophers than myself are of the same opinion) that the vast expansion of our knowledge of the natural world in the last century or century and a half, so far from weakening the traditional argument from design, has made it much stronger than it could have appeared in the days of Hume and Voltaire and Kant.'[a]

A thinker could not pursue any research if he did not presuppose that the world was a unity and had a meaning. He sets himself to understand more of its laws because he knows it is law-abiding. He may have no belief in God, but he nevertheless uses his brain with confidence as an instrument for assessing and verifying his conclusions. He may discount a superior Mind, but he could not work at all if he did not believe his own mind functioned in a coherent and purposive manner. And thus before he begins to work he has to assume a rational world and to employ reason to elucidate its orderly significance. It is passing strange if he believes that such Reason came without any reason. He depends upon the orderliness of his own mind and the orderliness of nature, and must treat logic with great violence if he still asserts that such coherence sprang from incoherence and out of chaos, cosmos rose. There is purposive adaptation not alone in organic but in human nature. 'We look before and after, and pine for what is not.'[b] 'Abraham, when he was called to go out into a place which he should after receive for an inheritance, obeyed; and he went out, not knowing whither he went. . . . For he looked for a city which hath foundations, whose builder and maker is God.'[c] The pattern of men's conduct is shaped by their expectations. Indeed, it may be said that the more finely evolved the type, the more does a purposive adaptation to life involve the seeking of ends not wholly to be fulfilled in a space-time order. The true scientist obedient to his desire for truth, and inflexible in his integrity, is not concerned with his own greater wealth or comfort. He conducts his researches (at least in part) because he desires to open more fully

---

[a] *Does God Exist?*, p. 57.   [b] Shelley, *To a Skylark*.   [c] Hebrews 11[8-10].

our understanding of the universe. To that degree his work has a future reference. Life moves on because men look forward. The reformer dreams of a world free from want and fear and the Christian walks by faith in the city of brotherly love. Their brethren scoffed at Joseph because he was a dreamer, but in the end they came as suppliants to him. For without the power to dream men are without a spur to action. The instinctive adaptation of creatures to future ends makes life possible, but the conscious adaptation of man to highest ends makes life noble. We move out of the old haunts restlessly because we are stirred 'by the hope of the City of God at the other end of the road'.

The thinker addresses himself to his particular task because he assumes reason and order and purpose at the heart of things. In a word, the design commends itself as reasonable, orderly, and purposive. Einstein said that if he did not believe in the regularity of Nature's sequences he could take no further interest in physics. The more extensive the research, the more intricate and amazing the pattern becomes, but it remains a pattern. The non-believer must explain the pattern as he is able, but to the believer no such difficulties exist. Since there is God, and since He is at work, history has meaning, and the world shows a pattern that is not static but dynamic. He knows that organic as well as inorganic nature is upheld by law. He gladly accepts the laws of physics, but he believes equally there are laws in metaphysics. God would not be God if He had a design for His world, but no design for His children living in it. Paul dared to say that there was a single end in God's creative purposes. 'The creation waits with eager longing for the sons of God to be revealed.' Part of the pattern is seen by the scientist, but part also by the theologian. If God has His plan in nature, He also has His plan in human nature, and in the history of the one world that one purpose is unfolded. Francis Thompson declared:

All things by immortal power,
Near or far,
Hiddenly
To each other linked are,
That thou canst not stir a flower
Without troubling of a star.[a]

[a] *The Mistress of Vision.*

In this indivisible truth of God, the theologian discovers that part which bears upon God's scheme for man. The difference between those people quoted so often by Sir James Frazer in his *Golden Bough* as committing most evil practice in the name of religion; and ourselves, observing normally a civilized code, is not so remarkable as the fact that both of us possess a moral consciousness, and distinguish right from wrong. Doubtless Frazer was right, and the priests at Nemi guarding the mistletoe were foredoomed to the sacrificial knife, and doubtless also we hang a man who murders another. But the devotees of that dark cult had their code of right and wrong, just as the cannibal feeding on human flesh also keeps his moral imperatives and prohibitions. The first great fact of human behaviour is not that men draw a different line between right and wrong, but that they draw a line at all. Kant saw the presence of a purposive Mind because of the moral law within. We use the word 'ought' because as moral beings we are conscious of an inner compulsion. There are things we ought, or ought not to do, quite independently of present happiness or advantage. If we disregard this inner directive, there is a judgement of condemnation we pass upon ourselves. If we follow it, there is a judgement of approval. Professor W. R. Sorley argued that the eternal validity of this law of right and wrong carries with it the recognition of a supreme intelligence who does not need progressively to become acquainted with it, but needs to possess it fully, and unlike ourselves with our imperfect wills, is guided by it wholly in all its workings.[a]

But the argument goes a step farther. God designs us, as we are able, to apprehend His purposes and to engage with Him in their workings. He made us moral beings, and endowed us with the right of choice, because he intended us to live the good life in creative fellowship. It is this purpose which gives meaning to history, and significance to its countless separate events. But what is this good life and how is it to be lived? God seeks in history to communicate Himself to us, as men seek also to grapple with God. It is, however, obvious that only in slow degrees can He teach us and only slowly we can learn of Him. In the Old Testament, supremely, but also in the records of other modes of thought and civilizations, we can see the evolving apprehension of God's purpose in history. It is the Christian belief that there

[a] *Moral Values and the Idea of God*, Chapter 13.

was over long ages a *praeparatio evangelica*. Men's minds were being fashioned to receive the whole content of truth. They were adding to the understanding of God's nature, and His ways, not only in the commerce of social thinking, but by the inspiration of the great prophetic souls. In the fullness of time when the world and man alike were ready, God sent His Son, the express image of His Person, that men might know in time what He is like in all eternity. In the teaching of Jesus, lit up and interpreted in His life and death and rising again, we not only see God, but know God's plan for His creatures.

Does this mean that whilst the scientist follows an endless quest, the theologian, by revelation, has discovered his part of the great design? Must the scientist still explore, and the theologian only interpret? To talk in this fashion is to simplify to the point of absurdity. The scientist is not for ever discovering fresh laws, and making startling pronouncements. Much of his thinking must proceed within a certain framework. He has a vast corpus of unassailable material already to hand, and his work is largely that of using rightly the data he possesses, extending its reference and applying it to practical use. To that degree the theologian and the scientist employ a similar technique. The Christian thinker is in completer possession of God's design for man. But what he has received must first be assimilated and understood. He must extend its reference to every field of human behaviour and he must ceaselessly learn to apply it. The revelation in Christ since it is timeless in essence is general in its statement. Each age must bring its own apparatus to bear upon it and seize its message for that age. Within those principles, taught and illumined by Christ, a thousand thousand patterns of behaviour remain to be discovered; lesser laws within greater laws, and always with the changing modes of human society, there is need for the fresh application of Christian truth.

But this can joyously be done once it is realized that we are not doomed to slave on a meaningless treadmill under the unseeing eye of Fate. There can be no greater contrast than that between the man who, believing in God, becomes a fellow worker with Him in the fulfilment of a divine plan, and the man, who unaware of a controlling Mind, sees no divine intention in the world. There is a revealing sentence flung out of the heart of the Old Testament. The stars in their courses fought against Sisera. Sisera had opposed himself to the purposes of

God and all the universe was leagued against him. The counterpart to that prophetic discernment is the blinding vision of Saul on the Damascus road and the words which smote his very soul. 'Saul, Saul, why persecutest thou me? It is hard for thee to kick against the goad' (R.V.). Here implicit in both cases is the declaration that God has a plan, and if a man defies that plan it is the man who suffers. The *Titanic* was called the unsinkable ship, but when it struck an iceberg it was the *Titanic* that sank and the iceberg that remained. James Russell Lowell says in *The Biglow Papers*:

> *An' you've gut to git up airly*
> *Ef you want to take in God.*

We are accustomed to the notion of the world being tilted at an angle as it rotates upon its axis. But the Christian believes there is a moral as well as a natural bias in the world. It is tilted on the side of goodness. Plato, in his *Republic*, spoke of the prisoners in the cave who because of their position could only see reflected shadows, but knew that the shadows implied a substance. That is a figure of speech not unknown in the New Testament. We behold as in a mirror the glory of the Lord. We see through a glass darkly, and only know in part. Paul knew of the revealing of God's plan in the life and teaching of Jesus, but he also knew our limitations. Because of Jesus we know God's clues, but we so feebly follow them.

> *Beneath Thy feet we lie afar*
> *And see but shadows of Thy face.*[a]

Nevertheless, the shadows speak of the substance. The authentic Christian tradition, derived from older sources still, maintains that despite 'the dullness of our blinded sight' we can see God's purposes and pursue them.

This then is our halting place. History has a meaning. We are earth-bound and imperfect, but God has given us clues so that we may apprehend that meaning and co-operate in His work. We have argued that without God there can be no intelligible pattern despite the brave talk of agnostic humanists; but the purposive directive intelligence of God necessitates a planned world. For the Christian the argument is strengthened by the triune nature of the Godhead. God is creator and in the

a *Methodist Hymn-book*, No. 41 (1933).

words of Jesus, He worketh until now. Science has thrown its own light on this patient ceaseless activity of God. If God has formed the world after the pattern of His own thinking it follows that it will only work in His way. The origin of evil remains to be explained, but at least it is not part of the very groundwork of existence. As the devil is not the proud equal of God, so evil is not the independent contrary principle to goodness. The world is not destined everlastingly to be torn apart by two equal but opposing forces. Evil infects all life, but it still remains a parasite, and those creatures that it bodies forth, carry their doom upon them. For since the world was created and sustained by God it will be obvious that evil will bring its bane, as good will bring its blessing. Indeed, the reason why men discard evil things is that in the end they are seen to be unworkable. They create more pain than joy. They raise more problems than they solve. They are inimical to social good, and so in the end they are abandoned. In this way the Western world has cast off witchcraft, sorcery, polygamy, slavery, child labour, as age-long abuses not finally to be tolerated. A safe guide for any social reformer is to attack those evils which have already been exposed by life. The things that oppose God's purposes are known by their fruits. When men attack the commercial exploitation of the drink or gambling habit; when they oppose the settling of differences by the method of war; when they protest in industry and in politics against men being used as means, and not as ends in themselves, they are echoing the condemnation of the universe. They are declaring that because these evils are in opposition to God's purposes they result in public injury. And reformers in like manner give their support to those things that are manifestly in line with God's plan because they create happiness, solve problems, and make for public well-being. Since God is the Father who creates in love, there is a moral order which men defy at their peril, but support to their profit.

History has this enlarged meaning for the Christian not only because God is the fatherly creator, but because in Jesus, He has Himself stepped into the arena. The Incarnation means that even God can say 'humani nihil a me alienum puto'. God could take no more active interest in the world than to send His own Son to deliver us from enemy-occupied country, and enable us to share His victory over the powers of darkness; His victory over sin and death.

O wisest love! that flesh and blood
Which did in Adam fail,
Should strive afresh against the foe,
Should strive and should prevail.[a]

The work of God the Son was not alone to throw light on God's purposes, but to remove every hindrance to our co-operation with those purposes. By God's grace we are redeemed from the contradictions of a self-centred life in order that we may be set free to fulfil our destiny in the fulfilling of His purposes.

But in the Divine Society there is not only Father and Son, but Holy Spirit. We worship the God who creates and redeems, but who also energizes and directs the world and all its teeming life. The Holy Spirit is the pledge that we are not condemned to battle alone. We are not left comfortless. The Holy Spirit continually throws fresh light upon God's purposes and strengthens us in the execution of those purposes. We cannot see the whole design, but gradually by His strong pressure, we are led into all the truth. Despite our recalcitrance He unfolds the plan, and gains our grudging aid, until at last the will of God is consummated, and the pattern shown to be complete.

The Christian knows that history has a meaning because he worships the triune God. For this same reason he is assured that to those who love God, God worketh all things with them for good. It is this knowledge which saves him from a despair begotten of the sense of life's meaningless futility. Man is not a 'sick fly on the gigantic flywheel of life believing that the wheel is turned for his benefit'. He is called to see in history the working of the divine plan, and in glad committal of his life, to serve the high ends of God.

[a] *Methodist Hymn-book*, No. 74 (1933).

CHAPTER TWO

THE ONE KINGDOM

IF PEOPLE are engaged in committee work and their attention
somewhat flags, they are prone to scribble idly upon convenient
pieces of paper. Now the interesting fact is that the scribbling
resolves itself unconsciously into some sort of design. The most
complicated criss-crossing of lines resolves itself into a pattern.
Psychologists will give a technical explanation, but the habit
indicates the craving of the human mind for unity. The musical
notes must make a tune, the words must be resolved into sen-
tences, and the oils be used for a finished picture.

There are two angles from which to regard this disposition of
the mind. Do men try to impose a pattern on the universe
because of this urge for pattern-making? Or is it because a
meaning is to be found that men have been given an ineradicable
instinct to seek it? The Christian has no doubt of the answer. He
believes that life has significance and therefore history has meaning.

In a recent able book, Dr. K. R. Popper[a] strongly criticizes
the historians Plato and Hegel who in different ways sought for
this design in life. Plato saw the pattern to be perfect in the
heaven. The men in the cave could only see the shadows
reflected on the wall, but they knew the sun existed. We who
are Plato's cave-dwellers know that though we only follow
shadows, they are reflections of a substantive reality. Hegel
knew nothing of shadows. He believed there was an inexorable
dialectic within history, and so in the strictest sense he could
speak of the logic of events. It is easy to understand how Marx,
by standing Hegel upon his head, was able to use that conception of history for his own purposes. Hegel and Feuerbach were
the two greatest single influences that shaped his thinking. From
the first he gained his idea of a dialectical process and from the
other his materialism. The result of that strange marriage of
ideas was a grotesque creature called 'dialectical materialism'.
Ideas need not be true to move men to action. The mobs who
shouted in the streets of Paris the slogan of Rousseau that they
could grasp, 'Man is born free, and everywhere he is in chains',

[a] *The Open State and its Enemies.*

were uttering a double untruth, but it enabled them to find articulation for real grievances. And so Rousseau served their purpose and played his part in the French Revolution. Both the economic and philosophic theories of Marx are unsound, but they have served their purpose for men who had complaints enough but no words to express them.

Hegel's theory of history, ironically enough, has been used both by Fascist and Communist. It was twisted to justify both Prussian militarism and the 'inevitable necessity' within the historical process of Nazi Germany. For that misreading Hegel himself was partly responsible. The philosophers have pointed out the errors in his thinking, but for the theologians his reasoning about the meaning of history is vitiated by his wrong interpretation of God's nature and therefore of God's activity. Yet for the Christian there is a fundamental truth both in the views of Plato and Hegel. He is not afraid to be accused of historicism because he believes not only in the heavenly pattern but in its earthly unfolding. With Plato he looks to heaven, with Hegel he looks to earth.

The Kingdom of God is the heavenly vision to which he must be obedient as he strives to realize its meaning within a space-time order. A vision is not to be measured. It is not like Ezekiel's Temple, capable of detailed description. The Kingdom of God is at once in heaven, and progressively to be realized but never consummated on earth. The whole of the record of the Old Testament and the wider background of thought in the Ancient World foreshadowed the Christian revelation. 'In the fullness of time' is a rather decorous way of translating the much more breathless words of the evangelist that Jesus came in the very nick of time. When all the world was ready, God sent His Son not alone to reveal Himself, but also His purpose for the world.

There are two ways of looking at a mountain. The Everest climbers had the heartbreaking view of eternal snows, and a summit which seemed indefinitely to recede. The air expedition financed by Lady Houston enabled the airmen to look down on the great cloud masses and the endless wastes of snow. The summit was beneath them. In much the same way we have regarded the Kingdom of God as a mountain to be climbed; something lying in the distant future and only to be attained by unceasing effort. Men have sighed from ancient times for the golden age which shall usher in the years of peace. There is nothing distinctively Christian in the idea. Indeed, the Christian Church did not at first embrace it. Throughout the Middle Ages the Church was the Kingdom in practical effect and in much apologetic writing. But when the disruption of Christendom in the Reformation and Renaissance threw a greater emphasis upon man, the change in emphasis had far-reaching consequences. The sixteenth century was one of reformation and counter-reformation, of zeal in proselytizing and of new formations within the Christian Church. The seventeenth century marked the wars of religion, and consequent spiritual fatigue and exhaustion. Gradually as the eighteenth century wore on, the fallow soil produced another harvest. In the nineteenth century the Christian knew his standing in God's sight, rejoiced in his proper worth, and was confident he could bring in the age of gold. Quite apart from his own religious development he was affected by the thought-forms of his age. In the western hemisphere it was an age of increasing prosperity. In England especially, the fifty years' lead in industrialization and the expansion of overseas trade begot confidence in the guiding hand of destiny. The 'lesser breeds' were generously associated in that ultimate enjoyment of God's bounty which all would enjoy when the Kingdom fully came. It was a century of terrifying contrasts, but the poor knew their place. It was the well-to-do who looked around and expressed their gratification. When Darwin spoke of evolution, it had to men's minds infinitely more significance than a term in biology. It was the magic key which fitted every lock. 'Evolution', said John Morley, 'is not a force but a process, not a cause but a law.'[a]

Even those Christians who most feared evolution, and resisted it to the death as an attempt to explain God's workings in His universe were strongly influenced by it in their interpretation of the Kingdom of God. Mankind was surely coming out of the jungle into the city, and why not therefore into the City of God? Tennyson spoke of

> The great world's altar-stairs
> That slope thro' darkness up to God.[b]

In a verse which became famous because it expressed so perfectly the sentiments of his contemporaries he dreamed of

> . . . one far-off divine event,
> To which the whole creation moves.[c]

[a] On Compromise.   [b] In Memoriam, lv.   [c] ibid., Conclusion, xxxvi.

The theological liberals changed the poetry into prose, but their sentiment was the same.

Albert Schweitzer divided critical works on Jesus and His teaching into five schools: (1) rationalist, (2) mythological, (3) imaginative, (4) liberal, and (5) eschatological. It was to disperse the pipe-dreams of the liberal school that J. Weiss wrote his *Preaching of Jesus about the Kingdom of God.*[a] Here in boldest form was stated the catastrophic nature of the divine intervention, the destruction of the existing order, and the new world as the main elements of our Lord's teaching. Schweitzer himself belongs to this school, and his *Quest of the Historical Jesus* was epoch making in the history of Biblical criticism.[b] Nevertheless, despite his eschatological views shared in this country by F. C. Burkitt, it needed the sword and not the pen to transform the Christian's outlook. It was not until the shock of a world war with its aftermath of hunger and misery, begetting disillusionment and despair, that men turned at last from an evolutionary Kingdom of God. They had grown weary of climbing a mountain whose summit could never be reached.

The time at last was ripe for people to accept the idea that they could look down upon the mountain from above. Realized eschatology was popularized in England by the works of Professors C. H. Dodd and W. Manson. Professor Dodd in particular taught men not to expect the Kingdom at some unascertained future date, but here and now in the welcome present. Certain features were held in common with the revived Calvinism on the Continent. The emphasis was no longer on the work of man but the mighty acts of God. Deliverance was to come from Him. 'Not of ourselves—it is the gift of God.' The words had meaning in Norway and Sweden, Switzerland and Germany, in England and America. There is a difference of emphasis between Scandinavian, German Protestant theology, and the work of English and American theologians. Nevertheless, the teaching of a realized Kingdom, in common with Continental teaching, added depth to the idea of God and of man. It sprang from the maturer thinking of apocalyptic days. It is fashionable to think of that teaching as dated in the ever-changing emphasis of theological thought. But of theology it can truly be said: '*Plus ça change, plus c'est la même chose.*'[c] In other fields of thought new discoveries

---

[a] 1892.   [b] See also *Mysticism of St. Paul*, Chapters 13 and 14.
[c] Alphonse Karr, *Les Guêpes*, vi. (January, 1849).

mean a total change of outlook. 'Time makes ancient good uncouth.'[a] But the distinctive and (as we should say) supernatural feature of historical theology is that in essentials it has remained the same. In all Christian Communions the Apostles' Creed and the Nicene Creed can be recited with one voice, and Christians can unite whole-heartedly in the *Te Deum Laudamus*. Even an emphasis is, in fact, only a re-emphasis. In differing phrase it has been said before. If in the margin of more pleasant days men turn to some other aspect of Christian truth, this stress on a present Kingdom will not thereby become invalidated. It is a part of the enduring Revelation not to be disturbed by every passing wind.

Professor C. H. Dodd has set this matter on a Biblical basis. Jesus came preaching the Gospel of the Kingdom of God, and the first public announcement was to His own people in the Nazareth synagogue. In startled silence they heard Him say the prophecy of Isaiah was at last fulfilled in His own mighty works—and by signs and wonders they would know that the Kingdom had come. The Kingdom could not be attained by hard endeavour. There must be, as in the case of the Rich Young Ruler, the casting away of any bauble that prevented one grasping the greater prize. A repentance that signified a turning from self to God and a child-like faith in God's grace were the essentials of entrance. Except, in your willingness to commit yourselves trustingly to God, you become as little children, you shall not enter. There is nothing weak or passive about this surrender. The Kingdom of God suffers violence, and the violent take it by storm. Nevertheless, the violence is not the laying siege to a city, for the city's gates are already open. It is rather the complete emptying of oneself that one may be filled with all the fullness of God. For the Kingdom does not come to the stout in heart but only to the meek in spirit. It is the Father's good pleasure to give us the Kingdom. To his critics Jesus could say that if by the finger of God He cast out devils then had the Kingdom come upon them. And on another occasion He said to the unfriendly that the Kingdom of God was in their very midst (ἐντός ὑμῶν), which has equal truth when translated the Kingdom of God is within you. This Kingdom is like a treasure hid in a field for which all else must be sold. It is a pearl of great price beside which other pearls are as nothing. It is a treasury

a James Russell Lowell, *The Present Crisis.*

C

from which a man may bring out things both new and old. It enriches, it enthrals, it satisfies. All this Charles Wesley understood when he wrote:

> *Jesus, if still the same Thou art,*
> *If all Thy promises are sure,*
> *Set up Thy kingdom in my heart,*
> *And make me rich, for I am poor;*
> *To me be all Thy treasures given,*
> *The Kingdom of an inward heaven.*[a]

The acceptance of the Kingdom as a present possession does not jeopardize other elements in our Lord's teaching. Jesus spoke of the fantastic mustard seed which, being less than all seeds, becomes a tree in which the birds of the heaven may build their nests. It is a leaven which though hidden in three measures of meal leavens the whole. The Kingdom therefore obeys a law of growth. How otherwise indeed can we understand our Lord's petition: 'Thy Kingdom come. Thy will be done, as in heaven, so on earth.' My early recollections include the schoolroom map of the world in which all the British possessions were boldly painted in red. We sang with fierce intensity, 'God who made thee mighty make thee mightier yet', and whilst we liked Elgar's setting, the words were better still. In all conscience the red blotches were thick enough, but our appetites were insatiable. It is in such romantic fashion that many conceive the Kingdom of God. The parts of the world in which the Gospel is preached are marked red, but they envisage a time when every other part will also be in red. A country like Afghanistan, in which Christianity has not secured the very slightest hold, is on this theory outside the Kingdom, whilst western Europe is well within its frontiers. God, on this showing, extends His Kingdom as more and more countries are evangelized. It is thus possible to have a celestial geography map in which Greenland's icy mountains and Afric's sunny fountains are special points of interest. But this is not the way to speak of the coming Kingdom. Even now 'the earth is the Lord's and the fullness thereof'. We do not need to wait for Reginald Heber's 'sea of glory to spread from pole to pole'. The whole earth is full of His glory. The map is already painted red. Afghanistan is as much in the Kingdom as Great Britain. The Kingdom of God

[a] *Methodist Hymn-book*, No. 349 (1933).

is not to be shown by the physical contours of a map but in the lives of men and women. The Kingdom grows as more and more come into the Kingdom. The growth is not to be measured from pole to pole but from heart to heart. For the Kingdom of God is the rule of God, and the Kingdom stands and grows, as more and more of His creatures own His sway:

> *The triumphs of Thy love display,*
> *In every heart reign Thou alone,*
> *Till all Thy foes confess Thy sway,*
> *And glory ends what grace begun.*[a]

No country can be called Christian but in every country where men and women love God and are responsive to His Will the Kingdom has its citizens.

But the apocalyptic passages in the Old Testament, Apocrypha, and New Testament are not to be dismissed. Schweitzer has made it impossible for any to neglect the large place of apocalyptic in our Lord's own teaching. Once, it was possible to deplore second adventism, as the sign of an unawakened mind. Even now the turning of the Bible into an *Old Moore's Almanac* is a horrid distortion of truth, and a regrettable deflection of interest into unprofitable channels. Of the day and hour no one knoweth. It is hidden from man and angels and even the Son of Man. Nevertheless, there is an hour known to the Father when the curtain is rung up and the play is done. We do not know the time or manner in which the Father will consummate the Kingdom. We do know that He will gather up all things unto Himself that He may be all in all. There will be the voice of a great multitude and as the sound of many waters and as the voice of mighty thunder saying, Hallelujah for the Lord our God, the Almighty reigneth.

Caedmon compared man's life to a bird which flies through a lighted hall and out again to the infinite space. So can the Kingdom of God be conceived. It comes and grows in time, but it neither begins nor ends there. Out of eternity, through time, and out into eternity, is the way in which we must strive to imagine what cannot be expressed. It begins with God and so must end in God. But of what lies outside our space-time order we know nothing. We can but trace the flight of the bird

a *Methodist Hymn-book*, No. 794 (1933).

through the lighted hall. The Kingdom then must grow, and yet we cannot end the work though we may co-operate in it. 'He speaks at length the final word, and ushers in the triumph hour.' The praise is His alone.

There are then three elements in our Lord's teaching of the Kingdom. It is present, it is growing, and it is consummated by God alone. But the all-important fact is that the Kingdom is a present reality and its wealth is open to all who would be rich. How could the character of God be otherwise vindicated? It would be intolerable, if like the slaves in ancient Egypt, we toiled to erect Pyramids which others were to see! How unjust God would be, if succeeding generations were to toil and suffer, in order that man in some remote future might inherit the promises. We would then be the drones whose lives were sacrificed for the sake of the queen bee. Doubtless, if men survive the perils of this atomic age, they will move from place to place at higher speeds. They will not be able to escape from increased comforts, conveniences, and luxuries. For the unprivileged there will be the removal of many hindrances to the good life. Poverty and want and even war may sometime be abolished. It is a consummation devoutly to be wished. But if all this came, it would not mean the Kingdom had come, and if all such hopes were blasted, it would not mean the Kingdom had delayed. In the play *Glorious Morning* the State official seeing the girl answer his knock at the door, clicks his heel and says, 'the State is all'. There is no response until in answer to his irate question she quietly replies: 'God is all.' He was able to point out with great emphasis that all that she had, she owed to the State: cottage and garden, work and food. Her reply was still that God supplied all those essentials without which the rest were as nothing. If the smooth working of politics and economics and science could bring us every material advantage we should still be without an answer to our deepest questions. Who are we? Where have we come from? What are we to do now that we are here? When we die where do we go? It still cannot give us a way to tread, or power to tread it, or the lights of home at the end of the journey. 'I have immortal longings in me', cried Cleopatra, and so much can be said for us all. Give us the four freedoms and still we are not free. Settle us in a pleasant garden city and we are still 'strangers and sojourners'. Even in the Promised Land of the Scientist we shall live in tents—for we are nomads.

It is necessary to emphasize our lineage because an all-too-prevalent heresy maintains that political security, economic prosperity, and scientific efficiency will give us the only salvation we need desire. The teaching of a present Kingdom refutes that heresy. However much these may prove mechanical aids to happiness, they do not constitute its essence.

All to happiness aspire
Only to be found in Thee.

The essentials of the good life are ours already. Men, a million years hence, will not possess more of the peace which passeth knowledge. They will not have more of that strength by which the world is overcome. They will not enjoy more of that love of God from which nothing can separate us. John Addington Symonds wrote of a time when a loftier race would arise with flame of freedom in their souls and light of knowledge in their eyes. In such an age they will be gentle, brave, and strong. High sounding words! But we can have flame of freedom and light of knowledge. We can be gentle, brave, and strong. The gifts of God are not conditioned by temporal processes. The heavenly benediction rests upon us all. Here and now we can know the grace of the Lord Jesus Christ, the love of God, and the fellowship of the Holy Spirit. It was for a people who were largely slaves and the children of slaves that Paul prayed that they might be filled with all the fullness of God. These despised people were fellow citizens with the saints and of the very household of God.

It was a clever Greek who first fathered the theory that history repeats itself in cycles, and for nearly three thousand years that idea has retained its power to fascinate thinkers. Perhaps the greatest modern protagonist was Spengler, who used the theory to show how inevitable was the collapse of our present civilization. But the Christian is delivered from a nostalgia for the past or a straining for the future. He does not think in circles. It is in the present that he walks in God's Kingdom. He knows that all things are his and he is Christ's and Christ is God's.

CHAPTER THREE

THE ONE BATTLE-FRONT

THE PURPOSE of God becomes plainer when one is delivered from the mirage of utopianism into the Christian conception of a God whose kingly rule extends over all, but whose gifts must be received by each. The Kingdom grows, as more and more become aware of its nature, and accept the conditions of entrance. The end of all things is not therefore the Mohammedan's picture of Paradise. The whole creation groaneth and travaileth until now, not waiting for extra speed, luxury, and comfort, but waiting for the revealing of the sons of God. Out of our new relationship with God, new standards of living may be attained, but they will be a consequence and not the goal itself. But to bring men to accept God's rule in their hearts, means not alone the work of evangelism, but of social service. Aristotle spoke of the State as making possible the conditions of the good life whilst the Utilitarians preferred to speak of removing hindrances to the good life. It is the same idea expressed in different ways. Is it not the State when properly functioning that can fulfil the eloquent words of Isaiah: 'Prepare ye the way of the Lord, make straight in the desert a highway for our God. Every valley shall be exalted, and every mountain and hill shall be made low: and the crooked shall be made straight, and the rough places plain'?[a] After this preparatory work, said the prophet: 'the glory of the Lord shall be revealed, and all flesh shall see it together.'[b]

In his discussion of the Christian Ethic as an Economic factor, Lord Stamp enunciated the constant and variable factors and showed that Christian principles could only influence certain social and human but none of the natural factors in Economics.[c] This is true, and Lord Stamp had no difficulty in proving it, but the Christian ethic in politics, sociology, and economics, must be weighed in a different pair of scales. By its operation in these three spheres the hindrances to God's fuller coming into men's hearts are removed. The crooked is made straight and the rough is made plain. The Christian ethic, as applied to public life, is not susceptible of precise definition, but three ideas are always

a 40³⁻⁴.   b 40⁵.   c *The Christian Ethic as an Economic Factor* (Epworth Press, 1926).

present: (1) All is subject to the sovereign will of God; (2) Nothing can justly be done which fails to treat a man as an end in himself; (3) There can be no overriding of the social good by a particular interest. The first is a preservative against any totalitarianism whereby the Crown rights of God are impugned. The second is a bulwark of individual liberty. The third secures the common well-being against the threat of private ends. Legislation framed in the light of these principles does not make good men, but makes it easier for men to be good.

There are some who being freed from the menace of Nazi and Fascist tyrannies are apt to suppose that democracy will make straight in the desert a highway for our God. Democracy would seem to be a term that all can understand. America, Russia, and Britain all pride themselves on being democracies, but if some unwary visitor from another planet supposed they meant the same thing, what a shock he would have when he landed in the three countries! Even if one tried to suggest they were three types of democracy and that the U.S.A. practised an individualist, Britain a social, and Russia a State democracy, it would only be an evasion of the issue. For the differences are not in degree but in kind. Any working definition would have to include the ideas of freedom and of representation in Government. But could the American President, the British Prime Minister, and the Russian Generalissimo smile happily in complete agreement over the meaning of those words?

The case is even more serious. Do people even within the same country nod sagely over an agreed definition? In Russia, who knows? There, people must publicly agree or privately suffer. In America the original draft of Government drawn up in the later eighteenth century still presses its largely individualistic philosophy upon a people living in a collectivist age. But loudly from the economic field and quite distinctly from the political field the cry goes up—how long?

In Britain the differences do not just follow party alignments. When Mr. Bevin spoke darkly of some Labour back-benchers as being crypto-communists, he doubtless implied they were more of a nuisance than many who form His Majesty's opposition. But do the young Tory democrats always applaud Mr. Churchill's eighteenth-century Whiggism? And have all the Liberals followed a call to separate themselves from socialism and to line up behind the opposition?

Now confusion in the ranks of Tuscany is not a vital matter. It is in the Government of the day that one needs the settled policy that comes from a settled philosophy. They at least must agree on their terms. It is quite arguable that disagreement over strategy does not imply disagreement in principle and that low-voiced grumblings over foreign affairs have not disturbed the general approval of domestic policy.

Nobody desires that the Government should be bound by rigid liberal obedience to the past. The 'socialization of the means of production, distribution, and exchange' was a mouth-filling slogan that at one time seemed to offer a classic definition of the Party's aims. But I remember quite an able speaker on the Labour platform who in the course of his address put his hand in a perplexed fashion over his eyes and said: 'What is that business about distribution and exchange? How does the sentence go?' It wasn't that he sought out the old chain for a fresh re-riveting. Not a bit of it! He was only going to use it by way of an illustration, and alas! he fumbled over the words. It gave me both amusement and satisfaction. The definition is too inelastic to be applied ruthlessly to the complex conditions of modern industrialism. Has a man got any distance when he defines capitalism as the system of private rather than State enterprise? It might be at once objected that there was no system, and that enterprise was at once public and private. The people who denounce capitalism, like the people who denounce modernism, ought to be made to define their terms. In both cases they are commonly under the hypnotic spell of word-association. Certain words have an emotional suggestion to which they immediately succumb. At this present time, if a Communist can denounce anybody who disagrees with him as a 'fascist beast' he feels good. The point is that he has given, to himself at least, a plausible explanation for an unreasoning prejudice. Many people denounce capitalism because in its connotation it seems comprehensively to sum up the sort of things they dislike. It is so nice to be saved the need of sorting out one's ideas, if cloudy impressions and prejudices can be dignified by a name. Every word that ends in -ism is a sort of rag-bag into which many ill-defined ideas can be packed. People give a war whoop and join in what is to their mind a holy crusade against capitalism, that evil monster. But, like the dreaded monsters of fairy tales, is it not a myth? A quite harmless object can throw a shadow that to a distorted imagination may seem grotesque and horrible. But it remains a shadow just the same.

Now all this does not imply that the industrial revolution and the consequent unregulated private enterprise did not inflict great suffering on the mass of workers. Beatrice Webb, in her splendid book, *My Apprenticeship*, has spoken of 'the small body of capitalist entrepreneurs employing at low wages an always multiplying mass of property-less men, women, and children struggling like rats in a bag for the right to live'. The slum mind, the slum property, the bitter memories, the class struggle, are all legacies of that industrialism which set the fat capitalist on the backs of the poverty-stricken workers. Nothing can finally relieve the sombre colours of that particular picture. A fifth of the people had initiative in production and four-fifths lost even the opportunity of it. The country prospered, but at the cost of its people.

But to condemn that savage cut-throat competition is not equivalent to the condemnation of capitalism as we know it today. The laissez-faire political philosophy and the Manchester school of economic theory both produced a reaction. A. V. Dicey has shown in his *Law and Opinion in England* the steady growth of collectivist thinking from the middle of the nineteenth century. The first Employers' Liability Acts and the Education Act of 1870 were early indications of collectivist legislation. Since then the State has assumed increasing responsibility for the sick, the aged, the poor, the disabled, so that today its 'grandmotherly protection' of the handicapped would cause Jeremy Bentham or any of the older Utilitarians to groan in despair at our indefensible softness.

It seemed at one time an unwritten law that you bought in the cheapest and sold in the dearest market. It was likewise axiomatic that no restrictions were to be put on trade. And in a world of constantly expanding markets the policy of Free Trade suited us very well. Herbert Spencer, whose philosophy seemed so vastly important in the latter years of the nineteenth century, could write of unfettered supply and demand as a natural law, and any sort of interference as 'artificial'. How great a change it is from the world of Adam Smith and Ricardo, Bright and Cobden, to a world of State interference with both trade and industry!

There was a third change, as the years rolled on, from the

early conditions of labour, helpless, in the presence of capitalist power. The workers made many false moves in the years between the Luddite riots and the Chartist Movement, but even before the mid-century a small group of pioneers in a Rochdale back street had started a movement which was to have world-wide consequences. The Webbs, in their monumental book on the Co-operative Movement, have shown that whereas co-operation and, profit sharing from the producers' end had an unhappy history of scant success or utter failure, co-operation and profit sharing from the consumers' end has placed the C.W.S. in a seemingly impregnable position. It was indeed her first researches into the movement and her contact with such leaders as J. T. Mitchell which gave Mrs. Sidney Webb (then Beatrice Potter) her vision of a Co-operative commonwealth.

Meanwhile the workers had sought their own protection from the rapacity of their masters. If some of the early Unions were too grandiose in conception to succeed, the idea of combination could not fail. Trade Unionism was the answer of the employed to the wealth and power of the employer. The great Industrial Unions are able to arbitrate with the owners of capital on equal terms.

Now all these changes from the earlier harshness of Indus-trialism have occurred within the fold of Capitalism. To say, therefore, that you oppose the present Capitalist order is to say that you oppose an order which contains within itself every graduation from the small shopkeeper and the private trader to the limited company, the combine, and monopolistic under-takings, to State control direct or indirect. Within a capitalistic society there is every phase between individualism and whole-hogged socialism. By all means say that you oppose the private ownership of capital, but to say that you oppose the present capitalist society just doesn't make sense. At this very moment in any large-sized area of population you may find the Co-operative Store next to a multiple shop and both of them near to the Town Hall and the Lending Library. The employer walks along a street that is municipally cleaned and jumps on a muni-cipal 'bus in order to go to the City Engineer's office or interview the Medical Officer of Health. If this criss-crossing of ideologies is true in our towns, it is just as true in our national life. Some of our most socialistic acts have been passed by Tory Governments.

In such a complex situation, any Government that is not

merely opportunist, living from hand to mouth, must have a
philosophy which issues in a coherent plan of action. It must be
able to define its terms. What does Democracy mean? Does
the Government hold to the egalitarian perfectionist views of
Rousseau, of Godwin, Tom Paine, and Bentham? Does it believe
the individual has rights which became inalienably his when he
contracted into society? Is it going to use its power to secure
effect for those views and those rights? It would be madness to
use a twentieth-century machinery of Government to enforce an
eighteenth-century conception of democracy. But if, via Robert
Owen, the Christian Socialists, and the Fabians, it has moved to
a more organic conception of democracy, what meaning does it
give to the 'freedom of the individual and his place in industry
and society'?

These are important questions because they will determine
the whole trend of legislation. But to these considerations of
philosophy must be added the necessity of learning from history.
Professor Butterfield has shown us in a recent book that it is our
wisdom to profit from the past by building upon it. We take
what we can, discard what we must, and then proceed to make
our own contribution. He demonstrates that the changes produced by violent breaks with the past bear heavy entries on the
debit side. They do not on balance show such gains as a more
peaceful and gradual method would have produced. This is
true even in such cases as the French Revolution, the Russian
Revolution, and the American Civil War.

Certain conclusions now present themselves. If the Government is to be guided by sign-posts of philosophy and history, if
it accepts an organic conception of democracy that does justice
both to the State and to the individual, and if it forswears an
abrupt break with the living tradition of British politics, it will
have no rigid scheme either of public control or ownership. It
will continue and even accelerate processes already begun which
have vindicated themselves by serving the public weal. When
private enterprise justifies itself on the side of production and
distribution, and does not injure the common good, it will not
be over-ridden in the interests of doctrinaire theory. But when
Industrial undertakings are wasteful, expensive, or dangerous to
public interests there is a *prima-facie* case for the most appropriate
form of State oversight or ownership. In one of his recent
speeches Sir Stafford Cripps said: 'We shall impose no checks for

checks' sake, but only when they are necessary, and as soon as possible they will, if necessary, be removed.' These are fair-sounding words, and history alone will record whether or not they were fulfilled. But if the three essential Christian principles for society are to be fulfilled, then changes from individual to public ownership will only come when historically, the time is ripe; when economically, the case is made out; and when philosophically, the method employed can be justified. Some objects of legislation commend themselves at once. Social Insurance, Housing, a national Health Service, a comprehensive and extended Educational system are all desirable, and vigilance is only needed in watching the method by which they are achieved.

If the Christian ethic must be applied in these ways to politics, it must in the second place be applied to the social conditions of life. When Goldsmith wrote his poem on the Deserted Village he focused attention on an ancient evil which had begun to show itself strongly in the eighteenth century and was to continue long after his death. The enclosure by the local squire, of the labourers' strips of land, made possible the divorce of the peasant from his land. The industrial revolution served but to hasten the process. The prospect of more money and different conditions of toil might in any case have been a compelling magnet for the discontented and the poverty-stricken. But the army of landless countrymen provided a ready market for manpower, and so the drift to the towns began. William Cobbett could speak in the early nineteenth century of London as 'the great wen', and the migration continued at such rate, that in our day Dean Inge has spoken somewhere, of the pimply red excrescences that lie around all towns.

This has not only involved a shifting of the balance of population. It has meant that industrial areas are overgrown whilst the agricultural areas are denuded. The recent economic depression only served to increase the number in the more prosperous towns whilst leaving the depressed areas to sustain their pitiful burden of stranded men.

We have, therefore, at the present time the problem of rootless people who have swollen the numbers in towns and cities, so that in the grotesque over-stepping of natural boundaries, they cannot be absorbed into a community life.

The physical aspect of such areas is an outward expression of the inner disharmony. The mean and drab appearance of the endless streets; the jumbled periods in architectural design, the sprawling formlessness of suburbs, added layer on layer without any interrelation, are so many pointers to a broken rhythm of life. Any pattern that once existed has gone, and with it a sense of community.

One of the commonest experiences after inquiring one's way in a big town is to receive the half-apologetic reply: 'I'm sorry I can't help you, I'm a stranger here.' One might easily suppose that every built-up area was composed of strangers. And, indeed, there is a vital sense in which it is true. For if people do not feel they 'belong' to a place by an inheritance of its traditions, customs, and outlook; if they live in it and yet do not share its life: then lacking a sense of neighbourhood they lack a sense of neighbourliness. They are 'like the chaff which the wind driveth away'. Can anything be more desolating in its loneliness than life in a great London suburb or in a huge housing estate? One never feels quite so completely alone as when one is in the midst of a large population who all stare at one with a blank uncomprehending gaze.

When people have no root they succumb so easily to the lure of mass mechanized amusement. They do not actively live; they are content to watch others live. They drop into the large and noisy 'pub.' They sink too often into a cushioned seat at the local cinema. They rush to exchange one novel for another at the circulating library. They throng to the nearby dog track. They live on top of their wireless set. And even when their recreation is harmless, it does not represent the best expenditure of their time.

They do not engage in social and public service. You do not find them on any voluntary or statutory bodies. They do not by their interest and constructive criticism provide any prod for their council. They may not even know their councillor's name nor the name of their own Member of Parliament. But how can they be public spirited when their home is their castle and the portcullis is always drawn?

But where there is no public conscience there is no effective check on those vested interests that would exploit the community for their own private ends. The brewers get their sites and houses; the promoters get their dog track; the cinema interests secure Sunday-opening without restrictions; the slum landlord escapes his deserts and unjust conditions in local industry remain unchallenged. Venality and corruption may creep into public life because no strong sentinel remains on guard. The local paper in its emphases and omissions may reflect the low level of community living. The few who give themselves to social and philanthropic work struggle against the heavy inertia of the uncaring. The salaried officials lack the incentive to high endeavour provided by an informed and sensitive public opinion. Representatives on public bodies are not forthcoming in sufficient numbers, and are not always the best qualified to serve. Contrast the surging local life in a town of historic traditions where people move naturally and are at home, with the lack of corporate interests and activities in those places that, having no roots in the past, are content to take none in the present. Dora Greenwell's words are most applicable. They are 'a waste, a peopled solitude'.

It is obvious that this phenomenon of rootless people in over-populated areas is a modern social problem of major importance. And whereas time is, in some instances, a great healer, in this issue it serves only to aggravate the disease. The problem must be tackled by the State, the Municipality, and the Churches, and both imagination and tenacity are needed.

It is easy to diagnose, but where shall the cure be found? However much one may regret the unplanned growth of urban populations, we have to accept the fact. Where extensive bomb damage has been created there is the unexpected second chance, and a gifted architect, if he is not baulked by sectional interests, but is supported by all men of good will, may find his daring vision become a glowing reality. 'A newer Athens may arise!' On the other hand, the community may not realize its swiftly passing opportunity, and the vision may be allowed to fade into the light of common day.

But the city that has been given no second chance to repent, can only free itself from the mute reproach of condemned and condemnable property, by using its powers to demolish, and then to create more worthily. It must use its powers under by-laws to acquire land and in this way, and by proper utilization of waste land, it must seek to provide playgrounds for children and for young people, and pleasant open spaces for the recreation and benefit of all. It is greatly to be hoped that those recommendations in the Scott and Uthwatt reports which strengthen local authorities in the creation of public amenities may soon be implemented.

There will still remain the necessity of dividing a large industrial town into neighbourhood groups of 10,000 to 15,000 people. These units must be provided with the apparatus of their own local life and every means taken to foster the 'spirit of good will and neighbourly regard'. It is not just a matter for the pooled wisdom of architect, town-planning officer, and city engineer, nor for the appropriate committee of the municipal council. It must be the concern of citizens within those units, who by voluntary associations and corporate activities make 'the dry bones' live.

It is a matter for rejoicing that there is now a Minister of Town and Country Planning with appropriate powers, and that the satellite towns planned for the future will not be allowed to become too large and unwieldy, nor to lack essential public services. But even these towns, the darling children of scientific planners, can only create the conditions of organic community life. People must see and approve and enter into the spirit of the plans, or else they remain for ever blue-prints of what might have been.

In the third and last place the Christian ethic must be applied to Industry. It will not be disputed that friction slows up the efficient running of the economic machine. The outstanding work of Mary Follett (*Dynamic Administration*) has shown the importance of a new technique, and whilst other writers have followed in her wake, industrial psychologists have confirmed her observations by practical tests. The title of Peter Drucker's book, *The End of Economic Man*, might be taken as the text for this school of thinking. Actually so far as this country is concerned, the sources of inspiration go back as far as John Ruskin and William Morris. When Ruskin declared in *Unto this Last* that there is no wealth but life, he gave to the industrial world a maxim capable of endless application. A platitude is only a truth well worn with use. Our familiarity with Ruskin's writings ought not to blur the fact that they were written at a time when, for many, life consisted in the pursuit of wealth. The fight is in process of being won, not solely because industrial capitalism, as Ruskin knew it, can no longer present a hale and hearty countenance in the changed economic conditions of this century; it is not even through the united efforts of the workers themselves, but even more because, given sufficient time, truth is mighty and shall prevail. Slowly it is being recognized that what is morally right is also financially possible and economically expedient. The narrow interests of the management and the larger interests of society are both served when workers are treated not as instruments of production but as men. 'Workers' Playtime' in the six years of war and now in years of peace symbolizes the new treatment of the nation's workers as persons in their own right. The old incentive to production were the stick and the carrot. But the war vastly increased the number of industrialists who refused to treat people as donkeys. New and better incentives were discovered. A truer understanding of human nature was shown. The teaching of the prophets began to bear fruit.

It was found that the environment in which people work can raise or depress their spirits. A cheerful distemper on the walls, and the intelligent arrangement of furniture and plant within office, workshop, and factory, just because they formed the whole background of workers' lives played a material part in shaping their outlook. The value of cleanliness, ventilation, warmth, and good lighting, had been recognized in factory legislation, but how great a gulf lies between the minimum legal requirement and the maximum effort of those with vision and capacity! In some industrial undertakings the change from the old order to the new was like the safety curtain in the pantomime before which two men speak, and then with the lifting of the curtain comes the breath-taking 'transformation scene'. Playing-fields, well-appointed canteens, rest-rooms, first-aid posts, and whatever else promotes material well-being are recognized at least in larger concerns as the background to the worker's life. In some instances these physical provisions are supplemented by music, entertainment, or talks in the canteen during the lunch interval, and in co-operative recreational and cultural activities outside the working-hours. In the early war years a disused railway tunnel attracted many hundreds of Bristol people during the heavy air-raids and the nerve-wracking summonses of the sirens. Lamps and candles threw a fitful uncertain light on men, women, and children perching upon their improvised chairs, avoiding the drops which in many places percolated through roof and walls, and striving to banish their fears by discussing what Lord Haw Haw intended and what the future foreboded. Then there came municipal action. The walls and roof were strengthened and protected from damp. Electric light banished the dark shadows, and grandma had a bunk and not a chair in which to sleep. The cheerful appearance of the walls, the rows of well-made bunks, the boarded floor, and an open space for meeting or concert, were physical changes which at once created a new mental climate. When a canteen was installed and volunteers were needed to assist, a community life sprang up at once. Gone was the old gloom of shelter and gone the old gloom of spirit. The city authorities doubtless began to have a new worry. These people who assisted each other cheerfully in the common life of the shelter were in danger of becoming contented cave dwellers. To act as their unofficial Padre gave me the opportunity of recognizing the immense psychological difference which a change in physical surroundings can produce. But even more impressive was the spiritual value of the canteen. It stood as the symbol of a new communal life in which the users of the shelter behaved as members of the one family.

It is not otherwise in any place of work. The improvement of material conditions is a first step, but even more important is the change in mental outlook. The experiment in applied industrial psychology conducted at the Hawthorne works of the Western Electric Company, U.S.A. (1924–32), is now very generally known. The firm began a series of experiments in which the workers' co-operation was secured. Hours were shortened, and other material benefits one by one were introduced. Meanwhile the reactions of the employees as well as the rate of production were steadily noted. Then with the consent of the employees the favourable conditions were removed, and still output was increased. It was found that even shorter hours and better conditions were featherweights in the balance against the heavy pull of spiritual factors. If the workers could share in the social experiment they would remain unaffected by worsened conditions and output still would rise. Give them however better advantages, and exclude them from the co-operation, and with such a shadow on the spirit, production falls. In an investigation conducted recently at an engineering plant the managing director said that if anything goes wrong in the factory he blames himself. He said of the workers: 'They are not slaves, they have the team spirit, they are proud to do their job, that is why we get no rejects, no scraps. . . . I don't tell a machinist, Do this job for

D

me. I say, You and I are working for the same thing—the consumer, if you work for the consumer you are working for the country.'[a]

Industrial psychologists have been pressing this same conclusion upon employers for many years. If goods are to be cheap and generally available, mass production will be necessary and many jobs will be monotonous and repetitive. Charlie Chaplin in his picture *Modern Times* presented a scathing indictment of large-scale industry which has no body to be kicked and no soul to be damned. The all-seeing eye cannot only watch the hapless slaves of the conveyor belt at their work, but also when pressed by inexorable necessity they must temporarily leave it. Woe betide the unlucky wight who has not completed his part of the process when the product moves along to the next worker on the belt! Charlie Chaplin's solution was to show a fade-out of the film on the figure of the tramp with the factory gates closed behind him walking down the long road toward the golden sunset.

> *When the artless doctor sees*
> *No one hope, but of his fees,*
> *And his skill runs on the lees;*
> *Sweet Spirit comfort me!*[b]

Robert Herrick might well despair when he had a doctor who could diagnose but could not cure. To escape down a road may be good for one man but not for the children of men. We desire neither to be robots nor tramps. Eric Gill's indictment of factory industrialism was that it deprives a man of freedom, responsibility, ownership, and union. He said it unwearyingly in all his books, and the sting in his attack has not died with his death. He would not give art to the 'arty' because for him it was no embellishment to life, but life itself, as it consisted in the right making of things. He believed that the ability and enthusiasm for such work was part of everyman's heritage. 'Art', he said, 'is simply the well making of what needs making,' and again: 'Art is collaboration with God in creation.'[c] To be a tramp is to have a certain kind of freedom but no responsibility. To be a robot is to have neither freedom nor responsibility. When we talk of the goods made available to poor as well as rich by modern industrialism, and proceed to congratulate ourselves on higher

---

[a] *News Chronicle*, 27th November 1946. [b] *Coming to Christ.*
[c] *Art Nonsense and Other Essays* (1934).

standards of living for all, let us at least not be under any delusion about the price we have had to pay. And let us strive mightily, as we are able, to rescue persons from the tyranny of machines. 'If a man is essentially a tool-using animal, the tool is from the beginning that of the artist no less than that of the labourer.'[a] It is human values we must be intent to salvage. If a person has to do a monotonous piece of work, endlessly repeated, at least let him know his job in relation to all the jobs in the factory. What is more important still, let him know what happens when the goods leave the factory. Where do they go and how do they benefit the community at large? The little girl with the least important job in the vast workshop, ought never to be shown at once to her place on the bench, but ought to have an opportunity to know her part in the whole concern, and the part of the concern in the whole life of society. Workers in a word are persons and must never be treated as means to an end. There must be no 'bruising of the hapless head of a wronged people yearning to be free'. To stimulate interest and invite co-operation is both wisdom and duty on the part of the management.

But to say so much is to say so little. For many years certain employers have realized that more is demanded. According to the last official returns of the Ministry of Labour, in 1937, there were apart from the Co-operative Societies, two hundred and sixty-six schemes of profit sharing and co-partnership. Out of a total of three hundred and eighty-five thousand employed by such firms, two hundred and twenty-three thousand participated in the schemes. The Co-Partnership movement began in England with the shops set up by the Christian Socialists, 1849, but co-operation in production is much harder and more perilous than co-operation in consumption. Despite the gallant failure of the first schemes there have been later attempts at co-operative pro-duction,[b] but generally speaking the method, after working-expenses have been paid and reserves put on one side, is to declare a standard rate of interest on Ordinary shares, and share the balance of profits between employees qualified to participate and the holders of Ordinary shares including, where it applies, the employee-shareholders. No bonus paid out in years of pros-perity, or on the workers' output, is equivalent to partnership or

[a] Christopher Dawson, *Progress and Religion*.
[b] The Labour Co-Partnership Association, whose title was changed in 1926 to the Industrial Co-Partnership Association, has sought for over sixty years to promote active co-partnership in industry.

profit-sharing. There must be in addition to wages, a share fixed beforehand in the profits realized by the undertaking. The distribution can take many forms. In the largest scheme of all, J. T. & J. Taylor Ltd., woollen manufacturers, have during fifty-four years of profit sharing paid to their workers in cash, Government securities, bonus shares, dividends, and allocations to a Benefit Fund, over £1,000,000. Present or late employees own more than four-fifths of the capital, but their shares do not carry voting rights. Vauxhall Motors Ltd., after paying six per cent. on the net capital invested in the business through the year, distribute ten per cent. of the profits to their employees.

But however well the workers are rewarded, profit sharing only shades off into co-partnership when actual consultation between management and men is introduced. It is this development which, even more than profit sharing, is significant for industry as a whole. To improve physical conditions or to stimulate interest is excellent, but the ultimate aim must always be the free interchange of views between management and workers in the conduct of the firm. During the war years a notable advance was made. In 1943 there were roughly four thousand five hundred joint production committees in engineering and allied industries. Over ninety per cent. of the shipyards had set up yard committees. The building contracts of the Ministry of Works meant almost inevitably the setting up of site committees. In the coal-mining industry there were over a thousand pit production committees. The same story could be told in other industries. When there was need the relevant problems were discussed by regional joint consultative boards whilst trade union district production committees maintained contact with their local committees. This spur of common concentration in satisfying national needs sent up production in a dramatic way.

If the method brought such dividends in war, why should it not succeed in days of peace? There is no need to be scared by bogeys. Consultation does not imply the workers' direction of industry. James Burnham has stated a strong case in demonstrating managers to be the true rulers in the new industrial society.[a] In any case an indefinite number of hands cannot grip the steering wheel. But suspicion persists and joint production

[a] He thinks that the possible alternative of political Bureaucrats is largely a play on words; cf. *Managerial Revolution*, pp. 136f. (Penguin, 1941).

committees have steadily declined in numbers. Some employers undoubtedly feel that consultation may infringe the prerogatives of management. They wonder whether it will give opportunity to trouble makers, or prove to be a waste of time. And just as there are workmen who are inveterately suspicious of any move the management may make, and are always disposed to ask, 'What are they up to now?', so there are employers who seem congenitally unable to trust workmen and to value their counsel. Shop stewards are often near-Communist in sympathy, and joint production committees do not fit into their scheme of things, whilst trade union officials wonder how it will affect the bargaining prospects.

Even the Government seems more conscious of the difficulties than the advantages. In the national production plan no place has yet been found for joint consultation because according to the Parliamentary Secretary to the Ministry of Labour joint consultation is a matter which must be left to voluntary agreements in the factories. *The Times* (8th January 1947) has suggested that joint production committees might be brought under the aegis of the Board of Trade. This is a reasonable proposition because the Board has responsibility for stimulating production and these committees, when functioning properly, serve that same end. There are regional Boards of Industry which might be responsible for joint consultation at that level.

One thing is certain. Nothing is more essential than increased production, and the more the private profit-making motive is eliminated, the more necessary will be the need to encourage the workers to play their full and proper part in the economic recovery of the nation. We must recognize in Professor F. J. Roethlesberger's words that 'a human problem to be brought to a human solution requires human data and human tools', and that the social structure of any organization, industrial or otherwise, is 'an intricate web of human relations bound together by a system of sentiments'. This means that there must be joint consultation at local, regional and national levels. The one goal to which we must steadily move is the identification of interest between management and men in the service of the common good. Industrial team-work in the interests of society is no unworthy slogan for such a time as this. 'Government and co-operation', said Ruskin, 'are in all things the laws of life; anarchy and competition the laws of death.'[a] There was no class struggle, cried someone bitterly, until Marx discovered it. That half-truth does illumine the fact that there is no necessity for struggle within industry, but only for understanding and a common strategy. Last century the worker was on the defensive, and only through the Trade Union could he pit himself against the power of the employer. This century he is on the offensive, and is represented by a Government pledged to carry out a socialistic programme. How will the Giant use his strength? Is it his intention to dominate the situation? Unofficial strikes carried out against the will of the Trade Union concerned and holding the Community at large to ransom are disquieting symptoms of a willingness to fight 'for my interests, my whole interests, and nothing but my interests'. On occasion there has been not only this impatience with the negotiating machinery and the disposition to force the issue by more drastic methods, but a refusal to face hard economic fact. If a cake is noticeably smaller there is a limit to the size of the pieces that can be cut. On both sides therefore old suspicions and animosities need to be overcome. On both sides there must be the recognition that a changed situation demands a changed technique. On both sides there must be an effort both of will and of imagination, if industry is to be matched with the hour.

If in politics, sociology, and economics we can secure that right dealing which follows from right relationships, we hasten the coming of the Kingdom of God into the hearts of men.

> *He clapped the glass to his sightless eye,*
> *And 'I'm damned if I see it', he said.*[b]

If Nelson wants to see, then like any other man, he must fulfil two conditions. He must be in the right place for seeing, and then he must be willing to look. If a man is wrong in his political, social, and economic relations, it is difficult for him in that wrong context to see God and to worship Him. But when barriers have been overcome and a man is right in his relations it is correspondingly more easy for him to see. He can still raise a telescope to a sightless eye, but that will be a studied blindness. If a man is in the best position for seeing, the rest must

---

[a] *Unto this Last*, Essay iii, § 54.
[b] Sir Henry John Newbolt, *Admirals All*.

depend upon the man. It is the work of the politician, the social reformer, and the industrial manager so to change the conditions under which men live that they are brought to a place where they can look out upon their inheritance. Even then it will still be necessary for men to go up and possess the land.

CHAPTER FOUR

THE ONE CHURCH

IN THE UNFOLDING of God's plan 'all the body fitly framed and knit together through that which every joint supplieth according to the working in due measure of each several part, maketh the increase of the body into the building up of itself'.[a] St. Paul's metaphor of the body is applicable not alone to the Church but to our sharing of that travail by which His Kingdom more surely comes.

The reformer who attacks social evils is engaged in sweeping away those hindrances to God's rule in men's hearts. This is the justification for a resolute approach to intemperance, gambling, and loose sex-relationships. The test of the rightness of any social habit is by its fruits. Some habits are evil in themselves and recognized as such. The Decalogue derives its authority not as a fiat of God but because it is attested by conscience. There are social habits however in which rightness or wrongness is a matter of controversy. These must be subjected to the test of their effects on the individual and on society. When they arouse more misery than joy, more harm than benefit, and when they create more problems than they solve, diminishing and not increasing social well-being, there is a clear case for condemnation. The Reformer who pits himself against them is engaged in the necessary task of removing obstructions to the coming of the Kingdom.

Those who in the home, the factory, the town, and the nation, strive to secure right relationships, whilst working for the highest standards of human welfare, are engaged in creating those right conditions whereby the King can more readily come into His Kingdom. But the pulling down and the building up are only part of the plan. Social engineering is essential, but still other workmen are needed. The Kingdom does not fully come until the message of the Kingdom is accepted as the basis for living.

The proclamation of this message is essentially the task of the Church. For that work the Church has received its own special equipment. In his notable book, *Jesus and His Church*, Dr. Newton Flew has done much more than trace the Old Testament ancestry

[a] Ephesians 4^{16}.

and the New Testament description of the Church. He has re-emphasized with wealth of learning that the Church is not an organization but an organism; not made by man but conceived and inspired by God. For the work of the Holy Spirit is not alone in the individual heart but in the fellowship of believers, leading us despite our stubbornness and pride into all the truth. Even now by the movement of the Holy Spirit in history we can see the way we have been led and the work we have to do.

Everyone has the right to divide history into periods, and everybody else has the right to be on his guard against such generalizations. Nevertheless, I want to take the risk and to suggest that there are four great movements in European history; the Middle Ages, the Renaissance, the French Revolution, and this last period so hard to name, which dates roughly from the middle of the last century.

So far as the Middle Ages are concerned, the historian would say that they could be sub-divided and ought not to be treated as a single epoch. And yet, from the collapse of the Roman Empire until the beginnings of the Renaissance, nationalism, as we understand it, was not known. It is true, of course, that the Holy Roman Empire was more a symbol than a fact; the peoples of Europe rendered a very shadowy allegiance to the Emperor. But in theory at least, there was a unity which has not existed since. Philosophers, whether they called themselves Realists or Nominalists, were concerned with the universal. The Gothic style of architecture was designed to achieve unity by the perfecting of parts into an organic whole. Business was not a matter of individual enterprise, but of trade and craft guilds and corporations. In the greatest of medieval poems, Dante is not concerned with a particular person, but with universal man who is taken through the circles of earth, hell, hades, and heaven. The Middle Ages were still under the sway of Ancient Rome and therefore of Roman Law. Now the Stoics, thinking as they did in terms of humanity as a whole, had largely shaped this system of Law. The Law of Nature in the hands of the Stoics was equivalent to the moral law. It spoke of those common rights and duties which belong to all mankind. If the literature, philosophy, and jurisprudence of the Middle Ages was universalist in outlook, the unity of the age can be easily understood.

Charles Reade's book, *The Cloister and the Hearth*, is not historically accurate, but it does convey a rich impression of the

cosmopolitanism of the Middle Ages. Along the great highways
of Europe there jostled together soldiers seeking any who would
enlist their services, students going from one place of learning to
the next, and pilgrims travelling to the great shrines of devotion.
There were no rigid, national boundaries, no passports and no
high walls of tariff. Not as many people knew Latin as historians
once supposed, but it was at least a common tongue for educated
men. There is not much danger of modern man idealizing the
Middle Ages, but at least let us recognize the underlying unity
of Europe which existed in theory and partly, at least, in fact.

When we speak of the Renaissance we so often talk of the
revival of learning, or the voyages of discovery, or the invention
of printing and its consequences. But they are only aspects of
a much greater movement of thought. The Renaissance was in
fact the emergence of man. There was a shifting of interest from
God and the supernatural world to man in his present and
immediate world. In literature was shown a love of the table
and delight in clothes, a zest for outdoor pastimes, and a lively
interest in the pleasures of the mind.

A direct consequence of this revolution in thought was the
rise of the peoples of Europe into political self-consciousness.
And once they knew themselves to be nations, the whole medieval
structure of life was broken. The words of the Bishop of Beauvais
to Warwick in Bernard Shaw's play *St. Joan* are pertinent. 'As
a priest I have gained knowledge of the minds of common people
and there you will find a more dangerous idea. I can express it
only by such phrases as "France for the French, England for the
English, Italy for the Italians, Spain for the Spanish. . . ." To
Joan the French speaking people are what the Holy Scriptures
describe as a nation. Call this side of her heresy, nationalism, if
you will: I can find no better name for it, I can only tell you it
is essentially anti-Catholic and anti-Christian, for the Catholic
Church knows only one realm, and that Realm is Christ's Kingdom.' The Bishop was right. The emergence of nations marked
the beginnings of a new age.

But although the Renaissance broke down medieval solidarity,
it did not mean that individualism had triumphed, but only that
the process had begun. An interest in universal man was bound
in time to lead to an interest in men in particular. First there
came the nation, conscious of its power, and then later the
people within a nation, conscious of their power. This logic of

events can be clearly seen in the work of the political philosophies. Hobbes and Machiavelli were great apologists for absolutism. The interests of a people were wholly identified with the interests of the Ruler. 'The State', said Hobbes, 'is unified in the unity of its representer.' But later Montesquieu and Locke advocated a theory of limited Monarchy; and then almost inevitably, to complete the process, came Rousseau and Bentham expressing belief in a full-fledged individualism. That last phase occurred at the end of the eighteenth century. We speak of the French Revolution, and in our country of the Romantic Revival, but they are only aspects of this third great movement of thought which came at the close of the century. What was implicit in the Renaissance had now become explicit. The ordinary man had come into his own. In France it was no longer kings and nobles who mattered, but middle-class professional men, leaders of the mob. In the United Kingdom Crabbe and Cowper were writing of ordinary people concerned with ordinary tasks, and Burns in his poetry was true to his own dictum that 'A man's a man for a' that'. The period in which this full-blown individualism was supreme stretched until the middle of the nineteenth century.

Since then we have lived in the fourth great movement of thought and action. A. V. Dicey has called it an age of Collectivism, and perhaps that term is open to least objection. It does signify the swinging of the pendulum from extreme individualism. No longer is it asserted that each man must look after himself and the State must keep its hands off; but rather that the State must actively help those who cannot sufficiently help themselves. State interference on behalf of the child and the old person; on behalf of the unemployed and the sick; on behalf of the blind and the disabled, is not only tolerated but welcomed. Even before the war there was increasing Governmental control in industry, and this habit of looking at life from the point of view of the State rather than the individual is obviously growing. There is an extension, not a lessening, of the powers of the State and its control over the lives of individuals. We have in fact come to a point when we can consciously recognize ourselves to be active participants in another great experiment in the art of living together. What is more, we have for our guidance the lessons to be learnt from the collectivism of the Middle Ages and the later individualism. It is a process in Hegelian logic—thesis, antithesis, synthesis. We have to identify the individual and

State not in a mechanical but spiritual unity. In our own way we have to realize the noble dream of Edmund Burke of the State as a living partnership of the governed.

What has this to do with religion? The four great movements in political thought afford a very close parallel to the four great periods in the history of the Christian Church. In the Medieval period the Church had emerged from the ruins of the Roman Empire with its glory undimmed and its prestige enhanced. As the Emperor claimed the temporal, so the Pope claimed the spiritual allegiance of men. There was a most gallant attempt to realize effectively the unity of the Church. It was the Kingdom of God in visible form. Men took literally the saying of Augustine that outside the Church was no salvation. They adopted his imagery and looked upon the Church as the Ark of God. Within the Ark men were safe: outside they were at the mercy of the dark, engulfing waters. The Church left no place for individual judgement or inquiry. It guided a man through the long pilgrimage of life from the cradle to the grave. The price to be paid was the acceptance of organization, ritual, sacraments, and dogma. People like Abelard, Knox, Wyclif, and St. Joan, were troublesome and dangerous because they refused to do this. The Bishop of Beauvais said in Shaw's play: 'The Pope himself does not presume as this woman presumes. She acts as if she herself were the Church. . . . Has she ever in all her utterances said one word of the Church? It is always God and herself.' The retort of Warwick is that her protest is that of the individual soul against the interference of priest or peer, between the private man and God. 'If I had to find a name for it, I should', said he, 'call it Protestantism.'

In the Renaissance people came to political self-consciousness, and in the Reformation to religious self-consciousness. When people were no longer willing implicitly to accept what they had been taught but increasingly followed the example of St. Joan, the unity of the Church was broken and the Reformation resulted. This does not mean that the individual at once came into his own. Just as the Renaissance meant the emergence of nations, so the Reformation meant at first only the emergence of national Churches. In our own country it led to a Church of England owning allegiance to King rather than Pope. But a shattering blow had been dealt at the unity of western Christendom, and at least the principle of individualism had been admitted in the great doctrine of justification by faith. But as in politics, so in religion, the principle of individualism, once admitted, began to work itself out by its own logic. The close of the eighteenth century witnessed finally the triumph of individualism in religion as in politics. The Romantic Revival has, as its close parallel, the Methodist and Evangelical Revivals. For the work begun by John Wesley was merely the end of a long process. His teaching, and his brother's hymns, are an amazing commentary on the importance of the ordinary man in the eyes of God. Tom Paine declared the rights of man in politics and John Wesley did the same in theology.

But by the middle of the nineteenth century, individualism alike in religion as in politics, suffered an eclipse. There was a swing back of the pendulum. Now we are living in the fourth great period of religious thought; an epoch of religious collectivism. We are no longer undisturbed by various sects each claiming the right to speak of our 'unhappy divisions'. Indeed, we go much farther than that. We organize Ecumenical Conferences where representatives of different Communions within the Christian Church may discover their oneness in Christ. We have already, in this last period, witnessed organic union between great Churches, and we dream and plan for wider union still. It is a period when the claims of the fellowship, rather than the individual, are advanced, and Christ is approached as the Lord of all good life. Nothing better illustrates this religious collectivism than the paramount place given to the Kingdom of God in Biblical criticism, in Theology, and in our popular literature. But old mistakes must not be repeated. We need to reconcile the claims of the whole and the part; of society and the individual, and for that purpose we need to profit by the gallant failure of Medieval collectivism and Protestant individualism. The Medieval Church thought too exclusively in terms of the whole, whilst Protestantism has thought too exclusively in terms of the parts that make the whole.

There is a startling parallel in fact between the problem facing the Church and the problem facing the State. In both cases it is the problem of reconciling the interests of the whole with the interests of the individual. In the State we can move forward in one of two ways. We can either move to some form of totalitarian government or we can rest our democracy on a social basis. The first alternative is open to insuperable objections.

It is a rigid collectivism allowing no place for individual freedom except the freedom to follow and obey. The State commits the final blasphemy of making itself into God and demanding the whole allegiance of man. It uses every form of propaganda, especially education, wireless and Press, to that end. In consequence the individual is regimented from his cradle to the grave. He is forced into a mental and spiritual strait-jacket; and if he seems unwilling to yield this allegiance to an omnipotent Government, there is always over him the sinister shadow of the secret police or concentration camp.

If we are to be true to our rich traditions and heritage, so spurious a solution of our problem must be rejected. The democratic forms of government, bought at so great a price, must be adapted to the needs of this new age. The extension of the control of the State in industrial and social relations must be achieved without the rough overriding of individual liberties. There is an illustration in the development of political philosophy. At first philosophers spoke only of the rights of the State as represented in its ruler. Hobbes had no place for the people. For their own safety and highest good the people surrendered themselves to the ruler. The theory of the Divine Right of Kings was another expression of this belief. The ruler, and not the people, had rights, and his rights were not derived from the people, but from God.

But in the eighteenth century philosophers were thinking not of the Rulers, but of the people; not of the State, but of the individual. And so Locke spoke of individual rights—rights so fundamental and inalienable, that in extreme necessity they could even be exercised against the State. However, at the very beginning of our collectivist era, in the middle of last century, Mazzini cried, 'Not rights but duties', and increasingly since that date philosophers have not spoken of the State having rights over the individual, nor the individual over the State, but both having rights which ought to be identical. For if the State only has rights, there is despotism; and if the individual only has rights, there is anarchy; but if the State is the perfectly organized expression of society, then there is a general will in the realization of the general good.

This parallel with politics is significant because the same lessons apply to the Church. A single authoritarian Church compelling obedience and denying individual freedom, is clearly no solution of our problem. In the historical development of the Church men thought at first of the rights of the Church and denied the rights of the individual. Then in post-Reformation days they spoke of the rights of the individual believer rather than the rights of the Church. And now men speak both of the rights of the Church and of the individual. They are not set one in opposition to the other, but both are conceived as duties. The general will of Christians is needed to achieve the general good of the Church.

It is a paradox that universality rests on individualism. There is no whole community unless individuals recognize themselves, and are recognized, as parts of that whole community. In the fellowship of the universal Church, individuals must know they have an individual approach to God and their own particular place in His Church. Likewise, those communions which have been called of God to bear a particular witness, must still be able to bear that witness in the many-coloured life of the one true Church. A team does not consist of one single player, nor an orchestra of a single instrument. God fulfils Himself in many ways. The rich, creative life of the Church must be variously expressed. There can be a unity of spirit with diversity of manifestation; but each communion makes its offering to the whole.

Nevertheless, the great need is a vivid awareness of the essential unity of the Church. If men could have the vision splendid of the one goodly fellowship of believers, it would be an easier task to make it as actual in practice as in theory. There is need to make explicit the great message of the New Testament that the Church is not many but one. The metaphors by which the Church is described, all convey the sense of its unity. The Church is the body of Christ; it is His bride; it is His holy Temple. Now obviously the Lord has only one Body, and one Bride, and one habitation. There are diversities of gifts and of functions. The Church, since it is not dependent upon a Book or a Creed, or a Ritual or a Building, or a separated Ministry, for its existence, can be described in the New Testament as meeting in a house, or a city, or a province. Whilst Church labels describe the particular forms of Christian worship and dogma to us, it does not mean that other Christians are outside the Church, but only that they are in other divisions of the same great army. To fix one's gaze upon the separate parts is not to see the one Church which has its many parts.

The Church perpetuates the incarnation of our Blessed Lord bringing God to men, and bringing men to God. And since it is of God, it has His endowment. There is one Lord, one Faith, one Baptism. There is the one Word preached from the pulpit, dramatized in the Sacraments, symbolized in art and music and ritual, set forth in creed and dogma, expressed in life and service —but always the one Word of the one God. There is the one Holy Spirit guiding the Church into all truth. There is the one way to tread, which in the words of John, is the true and living way. There is the one Adversary to face, and there is the one victory over sin and death. And because the Church is one, eternal, universal, indestructible, there is for all believers the one ringing assurance, that against this militant fellowship of those who love and serve Christ as Lord, the very powers of hell shall not prevail.

We are familiar nowadays with the slogan that we must not think nationally but internationally. By that we do not mean that people must cease to have regard or pride in their own communities, but that their interest must not stop at the boundaries of their own countries. Narrow exclusive nationalism in politics and economics has proved a dangerous and mischievous doctrine, just because it is too limited in view. Men are called upon to be citizens not only of our own country, but of the world. In the same way, the time is past when Christians think in terms of their own particular Church body. The challenge is not to think denominationally, but ecumenically. All of which means that that loyalty to a particular Church does not disturb an allegiance to the world-wide Church. In the glorious words of Paul, we must know that we are no more 'strangers and sojourners, but fellow-citizens with the saints, and of the very household of God, being built upon the foundation of the apostles and prophets, Christ Jesus Himself being the Chief corner stone'.[a]

This is indeed a rich and inspiring conception of the Church. Whilst men for various reasons come into one section of the Church, they pass through that particular door, into the Church universal. They become one with all the followers of Christ in every age. They are in the same company and share the same traditions as Paul, Augustine, Luther, Knox, and Wesley, as well as the unnumbered multitude of unknown saints who in their day and generation walked humbly with their God. For they

[a] Ephesians 2 19-20.

belong not alone to the Church visible and militant, but to the Church invisible and triumphant—the great company of those who love and serve God on earth and in heaven. I remember saying once to a faithful parish priest: 'Don't you ever feel depressed when so very few come to your early communion service?'

'Few?' he said. 'Few? There are not only the communicants present—there is all the company of Heaven singing "Holy, Holy, Holy, is the Lord of Hosts"!'

Not in cynicism or despair, but with conviction, the Christian says:

> Like a mighty army
> Moves the Church of God.

For the Church is an army terrible with banners. The Church must move forward as one mighty army, but how is it to be done? For our encouragement, let us recognize that the process has already well begun. During this century we have seen important organic Unions of Churches in Australia, Canada, and Scotland. And only a few years ago in 1932 came the merging of the different branches of Methodism into the one Methodist Church. It does not seem possible for the process to end there. It is but recent history since a National Free Church Council was formed by such progressives as Charles Berry, Hugh Price Hughes, and John Clifford. Since the formation of the Federal Free Church Council there has been increasing fellowship and co-operation among the Free Churches.

The problem of the further union of Free Churches with the Anglican Church is more difficult because of widely different conceptions of the Sacraments and the Ministry. It can be safely assumed that a disestablished Church of England which recognized the validity of the Ministerial orders of the Free Churches, would at least bring union nearer.

It is by no means certain that the ultimate idea is uniformity of organization and of worship. The letter killeth, but the spirit giveth life. The one visible organized Church will be attained at too great a cost if it means sacrificing the rich varied life and contribution of the separate Churches. To seek it is an idle quest if it involves the surrender of dearly-held convictions for a mechanical idea of unity. That would be 'rationalization' achieved at too great a cost. The temptation must ever be

E

resisted to do in our way and in our time what God wants to be done in His way and at His time. Let organic union be pursued where it is natural and easily facilitated, and so let there be progress to larger unions still. The road is open to us, but the end of the journey is not known. There is an interesting parallel with politics. The conception of a world State which Mr. H. G. Wells has done so much to popularize, has been familiar to political philosophers in one form or another throughout the ages. The Stoics conceived of a natural law binding upon all men, and they thought in terms of world citizenship. But then, as now, the pertinent query is the form of the world State. Will it be a closely unified State or will it be a federated world State? Will mankind rest content with a world assembly and the sanctions of international law? And if the latter, what sort of federation? We do not know. In the same way a time may be reached when there will be a closely unified Church, or it may be there eventually will emerge a federated world Church.

The all-important point is not uniformity, but unity. If Christians can be of one heart and one mind and one way, the fitting form of organization will follow.

What is certain is that all Churches must be able to bring their gifts into a common treasury. There must be provision in any federated Church or federation of Churches for variety in praise and prayer and worship. There is equally needed the divine jollity of the Salvation Army and the holy quiet of the Quakers. And if room is made for variety in public worship and in the administration of the Sacraments so room must be left for variety in Church government. In Wesley's Conference in 1747 the following two questions and answers occurred:

Q. Must there not be numberless accidental variations in the government of the various Churches?

A. There must in the nature of things. As God dispenses His gifts of nature, providence, and grace, both the officers and the offices in each ought to be varied from time to time.

Q. Why is it that there is no determinate plan of Church Government appointed in Scripture?

A. Without doubt because the wisdom of God had a regard to the necessary variety.

As men work together for the advancement of the Kingdom of God on earth, unity of spirit may lead to closer forms of union in organization. If the Church is responsive, it will be led by God's spirit into all truth. Daring, initiative, and vision are imperative if the opportunities and the needs of this new age are to be met. But if the faithful are matched with the hour, the proper place will be found for the individual within the one Church which is His body: the great company of believers who worship the one true God, and share with Him the task of bringing all men into that Kingdom wherein dwelleth peace and righteousness and joy.

Since the Church is of divine origin, it is a unity. What we have to do is, under the guidance of the Holy Spirit, to become aware of our unity. Meanwhile the present task is not to bring together the separate Churches of Christendom, but to realize that they are one already. The Churches, in a word, have not to achieve unity, but to find the best means of expressing a unity which already exists. And for our enheartening there remains the striking fact that amidst all the changes of thought, Christians still repeat together the age-old affirmations of the Creed. In the course of the centuries there has neither been an adding to nor a whittling away from the main body of doctrine. Christians stand to sing the *Te Deum* and all differences are lost in the great truths which bind them together.

It is the Church, holy, catholic, and apostolic which the Holy Spirit uses as His main instrument for bringing men to repentance and so into the Kingdom. In this goodly fellowship there is confession and intercession and witness on behalf of all the family of mankind. In the offered prayer, in the reading of the Word and its interpretation, in the outspread Table, the needs of all men are lifted up to the great Mediator who ever liveth to make intercession for us. And not alone through its worship and its sacraments, but through its apostolic labours, the Church has brought men into the fold of God. If one had to describe in a phrase the difference between the world before and after Christ, it would surely be that before Christ men venerated the strong man in his strength. Since Christ came, men increasingly venerate the child in his weakness. In the old world the weak paid the penalty for their lack of strength. The race went to the swift, and the battle to the strong. Now a civilization is measured not by its treatment of the most powerful, but of its weakest members. The child in

the midst is in fact the standard of measurement. We test our
housing, our education, our industries, and our public services
by asking the one test question: 'Do they promote the well-being
of the child so that he has the fullest opportunity to live the
good life?'

Whatever our party alignments may be there is general recognition that in social insurance, town and country planning,
extended educational facilities, a national health service, attention has been paid to the least protected. In our legislation
human welfare has been the chief concern. It is due to the
pervasive influence of the Christian ethic that men know a
nation is judged by its treatment of the handicapped and unprivileged. For it is the Church throughout the centuries that
has through its witness and its message brought about this
startling change. It was the Church that first sought to provide
hospitals for the sick, schools for the ignorant, and relief for the
poor. It was through the social witness of the Church that there
came a gradual raising of the status of women and children.
It was Christian men and women who provided the challenge
to slavery and to intolerable conditions in industry. It is they
who have attacked great social evils in the face of misrepresenta-
tion, opposition, and ridicule. They have contended against the
unrelieved pressure of vested industries and the greater weight
of apathy from those who want to be left alone. It was Christian
men who so often were the natural spokesmen of the working
classes in their first struggles for industrial and political self-
expression. The Curtis Report and the Nuffield Report were
concerned with right provision for young and old respectively.
It is largely through the message and witness of the Church, and
of individual Christians within the Church that we live in a
society which cares for its sick and aged and unemployed. Christian people as individuals, and many Christian bodies, have
built houses for the orphan or neglected child, and for the aged
poor. The Government is sponsoring youth clubs and associations, but it is a work which the Church as a pioneer in the field
has been pressing for long years. Nor is it a matter of work done
by the Churches as a whole. The unfriendly outsider does not
realize the vast amount of work done by individual Churches for
the young and the old, nor does he know the great extent of its
community service, nor its influence on public life by the propa-
gation of Christian standards. When the sorry story of the

Church's blindness and obstinacy and conservatism has been fully told, it still remains true that the fellowship of believers in society is a leaven, leavening the whole.

It is to such a Church the Christian belongs. He takes his place in the goodly fellowship of apostles, prophets and martyrs. In holding fast the blessed truth of the communion of saints, he knows that the Church on earth and the Church in heaven cannot be divided.

> *The Church triumphant in Thy love,*
> *Their mighty joys we know;*
> *They sing the Lamb in hymns above,*
> *And we in hymns below.*

> *Thee in Thy glorious realm they praise,*
> *And bow before Thy throne,*
> *We in the Kingdom of Thy grace:*
> *The Kingdoms are but one.[a]*

It was the same Charles Wesley who in a vivid metaphor described the fellowship of believers as one Church above, beneath, and as one family with but the narrow stream of death flowing between. But even this stream does not truly divide, for he says:

> *One army of the Living God,*
> *To His command we bow;*
> *Part of His host have crossed the flood,*
> *And part are crossing now.[b]*

This is the heritage of the Christian. He belongs to the Universal Church which fills both earth and skies. He knows that to that glorious Church has been given the keys of the Kingdom of Heaven, and that what it binds on earth shall be bound in heaven and what it looses on earth, shall be loosed in heaven.

And therefore he faces an uncertain future with a certain hope. He knows that the saints are equipped, through the spirit of God, for the work of the Ministry, for the building up of the body of Christ till we all attain unto the unity of the faith and of the knowledge of the Son of God. The writer of the second Epistle of Peter knew that though the heavens and earth would

[a] *Methodist Hymn-book*, No. 818 (1933).   [b] ibid., No. 824 (1933).

pass, the word of God would not pass away. And in dramatic language he set forth his belief in the sure foundations of God. 'The day of the Lord', he said, 'will come like a thief. The heavens will vanish with a mighty roar, the stars will be set ablaze and melt, the earth and all its work will be burnt up.'[a] At such an awful time what might a reasonable man anticipate? The writer gives the answer: 'It is a new heaven and a new earth that we expect, as He has promised, and in them dwells righteousness. Then, beloved, as you are expecting this, be eager to be found by Him unspotted and unblemished in serene assurance.'[b]

That triumphant passage is the note of the New Testament as it is the note of the Christian Church. The house that was built upon the rock could not be shaken by the violence of the storm. And because the Church is founded upon a rock it shall not be moved.

> *In vain the surge's angry shock*
> *In vain the drifting sands,*
> *Unharmed upon the Eternal Rock*
> *The Eternal City stands.*[c]

[a] 2 Peter 3[10].   [b] 2 Peter 3[13-14].   [c] *Methodist Hymn-Book*, No. 703 (1933).

CHAPTER FIVE

THE ONE WORLD

'WHAT IS A Church?' said the honest sexton in Crabbe's poem,[a] and proceeded to describe it as 'a tall building with a tower and bells'. But Crabbe had a better answer than that. It is, he said,

> *the faithful, pure and meek*
> *From Christian folds, the one selected race*
> *of all professions, and in every place.*

That definition does justice at least to the different functions within the one fellowship. But the accomplishment of God's plan depends upon an even wider casting of the net. The Kingdom of God makes a call upon many workmen, each with his own particular part to play. How surprised Cyrus would have been to know he was the Lord's anointed and that God was upholding his right hand![b] There are many in every age who, all unknowing, are under the divine constraint and partners in the same plan. Rudyard Kipling called God 'the Master of All Good Workmen',[c] and so whilst the one Church is God's instrument for the proclamation of the message and for the spiritual sustenance of men, its task is made more easy by those who co-operate in God's purposes for society and create the right conditions for the living of the good life. The water-lily flowers in a mud pond, but that is no argument for saying the Christian life can be lived in a slum. Doubtless it can, but doubtless it is not God's intention that it should. How many are prevented from coming into the Christian life because of faulty education, unjust working conditions, the drag of heredity, and the coarsening effects of a bad environment. It is heresy, as we have emphasized, to suppose the Kingdom of God will come with good plumbing, decent houses, and higher standards of social living. But it is a more vicious heresy to suppose they do not matter. 'Your Father', said Jesus (in the matter of material comforts), 'knoweth that ye have need of all these things.' The evangelist and the reformer are both required. Change hearts,

---

[a] *The Borough.*   [b] Isaiah 45^1.   [c] *When Earth's Last Picture.*

says the enthusiast, and you will change conditions. But the process is too slow, and it does not always and necessarily happen. Dr. Lucock in one of his books said that if each man sank an artesian well in his garden, it would not give a municipal water supply.

We speak of a change of heart, but our Lord spoke of a change of mind. When a man is converted it ought to socialize his thinking so that he takes up a different attitude to his home, his work, his city, and his country.

> Father, Mother, and Me,
> Sister and Auntie say
> All the people like us are We,
> And every one else is They.[a]

But once a man becomes a Christian all the rest become We. Even when each Christian becomes a Christian citizen there is still needed the help of God's 'other workmen'. But how much more swiftly might God's rule be extended in human hearts if all the workmen knew their Master and their relation to each other. In a deeper sense and for a greater cause than any that Marx and Engels knew, we need to say: 'Workers of the world unite.'

The Kingdom is hastened by the labours of the many, but it depends for its actual growth on the acceptance of a message. For it is not a matter of steel and plastics: of ledgers and turbines. It can be designed by no architect and is beyond the reach of any builder. For it has its own foundations, and its builder and maker is God. The Kingdom can have no material realization, for it is the rule of God consciously accepted by men. It is the Kingdom of right relationships. The individual commits himself to an allegiance to God, obeys God's will and shares the divine victory over sin and death. But the acceptance of our Lord's mandate to love God and one's neighbour involves by implication the acceptance of the whole Christian Faith. For who is the God to whom a man surrenders himself? In Charles Williams's survey of Christian history[b] there are over forty references to co-inherence. The Christian faith is a unity, and Catholic and Protestant alike regard the Creeds as its authoritative expression. The God whose sovereignty the believer accepts

[a] Kipling, We and They.   [b] The Descent of the Dove.

is the Maker of heaven and earth. Of Jesus Christ, His only
Son, certain statements about His birth, life, death, and His
present and future work must solemnly be affirmed. The Holy
Ghost, who proceeds from the Father and the Son, is the Lord
and Giver of Life; and the one Church is both catholic and
apostolic. There is forgiveness and remission of sins by the one
Baptism, and for all there is resurrection and the life to come.
To say the coming of the Kingdom into a believer's heart involves
the acceptance of God's rule, is no bald statement involving a
plain decision. It invokes the pageantry of the Creeds, since the
art of commitment rests upon an understanding of God as He is
revealed in Christ and made known through the fellowship of
the Church.

The reality of that individual surrender is shown by our
willingness to serve Him. We are His friends if we do what-
soever He commands us. And so by necessary implication the
rule of God involves us in the whole range of Christian duties.
We stand in a new relation to God and therefore a new relation
to our fellows. Martin Buber has made us all aware in a fresh
manner that real life is meeting.[a] There are two primary relations: I — THOU and I — IT. I can only become I as I say Thou,
and to say that word is an act of my whole being. So to meet
God and so to meet my fellows is to fulfil the purpose of my
creation. Buber is a Jew, but his penetrating word is only fully
realized in the receiving of the Kingdom where a man hears God
say thou and when a man says thou to his fellow. Out of such
right relations, right conduct springs. The law was given through
Moses, but grace and truth came through Jesus Christ. An
external law demands continual observance, but the law written
on the heart is spontaneously fulfilled. A bad man for prudential
reasons may keep a good law, but the good man needs no
external sanctions and correctives. His good actions proceed
from a good will. The Kingdom of God growing in numbers as
more and more accept its King, exercises its own pervasive
influence on the lives of men. The extent of that influence is not
to be measured, nor can its effects be predicted. Jesus spoke of
salt and leaven, but who can detect the action of either? Yet
one truth stands out. The three great things man asks of the
future depend upon the increasing rule of God. Man asks for
world peace, economic prosperity, and individual freedom.

[a] *I and Thou.* Translated by R. Gregor Smith (1937).

The first great longing is for a world at peace, but this depends upon the recognition of God's sovereignty. In the process of history man has been brought through the stages of tribal organization to that of city States or petty kingdoms. Thence they have reached the stage of independent nationhood. But with the growing complexity of national rivalries, increased communications, expanding trade, and economic competition, they passed to a stage of alliances in which an uneasy balance of power was maintained. Further scientific discovery and technological advance made the world one. Cycles of economic prosperity and depression involved the whole world. Even whilst nations were striving for their own particular place in the sun, science and economics were making it impossible for them to live apart.

In 1914 two great alliances of nations fought each other, and by 1918 it was obvious that the only alliance sufficiently large to be safe was an alliance of all the nations. The League of Nations was a just outcome of events. It was a logical necessity in the development of history. It was a further step in the divine strategy.

But a further stage was still necessary. It had to be shown by the hard facts of bitter experience that a society of nations which was founded on the selfish aggressive instincts of mutually suspicious Powers could not hope to endure. It hastened to its inevitable breakdown in September 1939. But the failure of the organization does not mean the failure of the idea. The conception is imperishable. It merely needs a new setting.

If wars, ever more deadly, are not to be recurrent, we must break the vicious circle. We must not begin with ourselves; we must begin with God. However much we try to avoid past failures by a skilful re-fashioning of world organization, if we hope by agreement and discussion alone to maintain peace, we are lost.

If a company of well-intentioned burglars met to discuss how mutually they might surrender their tools of trade, what would be the inevitable result? Or to use a slightly more pleasant metaphor, if a number of highly civilized business-men met to discuss how they could drastically limit their profits in the interests of society, what would be the outcome of such a gathering? The plain fact is that if egocentric men, representing egocentric nations, meet with the best of intentions to discuss the common good, there will spring up again the demons of greed, self-interest, fear and pride, and the rest of the hellish brood, to frustrate their best endeavours. It is not just an axiom of theology, but of life, that natural man is unable to save himself. That fatal twist of the will and corruption of nature which theologians call original sin can never be resolved by the highest intentions and the best-laid schemes. The inner tension, the incessant tug of war, leads always to the despairing cry: 'Oh, wretched man that I am, who shall deliver me from the body of this death?"

It is for this sufficient reason that we cannot organize our own security nor plan our own deliverance. All the logic of events has brought us to that last stage in which, if we are prepared to acknowledge God as King, we shall discover we are fellow subjects; and since the King is also Father, that we are brethren. The Shepherds and the Wise Men did not find fellowship by discussion and argument. They came to the same manger and worshipped the same Babe and found that they were kneeling side by side.

But to reach that final stage demands a repentance which is a change of mind. It means that we acknowledge that there is no health in us, and that quite obviously sheep need a shepherd. Can a world society be built around the acknowledgement of God's sovereignty and His laws arising out of the ashes of this war? There are not yet sufficient signs of that repentance which makes men and nations become in their humility as little children, that they might enter into the Kingdom of Heaven. But if, in the striking phrase of D. R. Davies, history is a long-deferred term of repentance, the time may come when men are brought at last to see that only in accepting the plan of history and recognizing God's kingship, can a sure basis of world unity be found.

Men may of course resist. Niebuhr has underlined a patent truth in showing that with increasing cosmos there is the possibility of increasing chaos. Jesus spoke of the tares and the wheat growing together until the harvest. Only then could the tares be separated from the wheat. There are no grounds for easy optimism. Progress is only achieved by conscious effort and persistence. And always the enemy is at work in the field sowing his tares.

Nevertheless, though men remain recalcitrant, this is their destiny. And always there are individual persons who repent and believe and enter into the Kingdom and whose lives are fulfilled.

There has in our own day been a no more significant book in
its own field than Arnold Toynbee's *Study of History*. He knows
that as science is laying claim to the whole of spiritual as well as
the material universe, God the Mathematician is fading right
out into God the vacuum. But he has another way to what he
calls 'the sense of unity'. He quotes a saying of Alexander: 'God
is the common father of all men, but he makes the best ones
peculiarly his own.' Then he proceeds: 'If this be authentic, it
tells us that Alexander realized that the brotherhood of Man
presupposes the fatherhood of God—a truth which involves the
converse proposition that if the divine father of the human family
is left out of the reckoning there is no possibility of forging any
alternative bond of purely human texture which will avail by
itself to hold mankind together. The only society that is capable
of embracing the whole of mankind is a superhuman CIVITAS
DEI; and the conception of a society which embraces mankind
and nothing but mankind is an academic chimera. The Stoic
Epictetus was as well aware of this supreme truth as the Christian
Apostle Paul, but, whereas Epictetus stated the fact as a conclusion of philosophy, St. Paul preached it as the gospel of a new
revelation made by God to man through the life and death of
Christ.' Even now in the aftermath of war, in that extreme
weakness which can so easily beget fear and insecurity, there is
an international society in which all differences of race, tongue,
and class are transcended, and men know themselves to be one
in Christ Jesus. It is the one Church which makes possible the
one world.

The second desire of all men is for a world in which want shall
be abolished and the needs of all will be supplied out of the
resources of all. After the first Great War there was world-wide
unemployment, want, and suffering. To keep up prices, an
artificial scarcity was created in a world of plenty. God had
provided enough for all, and the resources of the earth were
multiplied by our methods of mass production. Nevertheless
food was destroyed, cotton reploughed into the ground, wheat
burnt, and fish thrown overboard whilst multitudes were starving.

In such an incredible situation man could only blame himself.
The economists had their explanation. They said that we had
learnt to produce but not to distribute. In simple terms it meant
we had not learnt to share. We were like the members of an
orchestra, in which though we had no conductor we hoped to

produce not sounds but music. We each attempted our particular solution of a problem which could only be solved by all
of us working together. We were like a football team in which
each member played his own game without reference to the
rest, and then we wondered why the score mounted against us.
I recall a small birthday party in which the table was laden
with good things and all the invited children might have eaten
with gusto and relish. But amongst the party were two small
boys who were determined to get all they could for themselves,
regardless of the others. The observance by each of passing the
plate would have saved the situation. 'Please' and 'Thank you'
would have made the meal a delight. But the boys would have
no such finicky niceties of social etiquette. They grabbed, and
when others to their infinite dismay saw what was happening
they grabbed also. And all was lost in the scramble for self-
sufficiency. The strongest had more than enough and the
weakest left the table hungry. There is no need to point the
moral of the story. It is a picture of the world between the great
wars.

Now men desire desperately to avoid a return to such insanity,
but they know that the same forces of greed, self-interest, and
insularity of outlook are still at work. And so they hope, but
they also fear. Right relationship to God, however, involves a
right relationship with others. If the Cross is God's method of
winning the world to Himself, we dare not choose a different
one. The sign and symbol of greatness is the towel and the basin
and the washing of the disciples' feet. The great paradoxes of
Christ's teaching gain in their effectiveness by the contrast they
afford between the accepted conventions of society and the new
ethic of the Kingdom. If a man ask your overcoat, give him also
your coat. If he force you to go a mile, go with him an extra
one. Do not merely love your friends, but your foes. If you
would be first, you must be last. He that is greatest must be the
servant of all. Only when you lose your life will you find it.
The teaching is interpreted in the life of the teacher.

The word of Christ is strictly relevant to our economic situation. The needs of all will be met by the resources of all when
we practise that ethic of the Cross which is the way of love in
active service. If we are willing to accept the principle, there
will always be technicians able to translate it into practical
detailed economic terms. There are disturbing signs of fresh

economic rivalry and the recurrent cycles of boom and slump. But the sky is not without patches of blue. Douglas Jerrold spoke of philanthropists who in a time of famine would vote for nothing but toothpicks. We have done better than that. The work of U.N.R.R.A. was prompted by many motives, and not all were idealistic. But if prudence and self-interested calculation entered in, there was also the influence of the Christian Gospel. The peoples have been fed and cared for at some cost, and to a point of sacrifice. The work of the Food and Agricultural Organization, under the inspired direction of Sir John Boyd Orr, means that the fluctuating periods of natural and man-made distress will be met by intelligent planning and by a certain control of prices and materials. The International Bank for Reconstruction and Development and the International Monetary Fund, together with the European Central Inland Transport Organization, are kindred organizations which approach their problems from a wider standpoint than national interest. In the winter conference of the Governors of the World Bank no serious disagreement arose, and the conference ended before the fixed time. U.N.E.S.C.O. both in Paris (November 1946) and in Prague and Geneva has made possible the fruitful meeting of intellectuals and the beginnings of fuller social and cultural life for all. Professor David Mitrany has said that 'the art of peace-making is not how to be skilful in changing the frontiers which separate the nations but how to establish new and fruitful points of contact, how to draw together the nations' living interests and activities across the lines which divide them on the map'. As one might have expected, the sheer pressure of economic circumstance is bringing us, however reluctantly and slowly, into that place where God would have us be. Economic history is showing us the relevance of the Christian message.

The third great desire is that the ordinary man shall come into his own. Even as men envisage an extension of State control and freely talk of a planned economy, they yet want also to preserve the rights of the individual. It is significant that though words such as collectivism, communism, and socialism are very much in the air, no word is used more than 'freedom'. It had almost been in danger of passing out of currency. Certainly it had become dull and tarnished, but now it has been brushed up and is more bright and shining than ever. The two sets of words with their two sets of ideas are being used together because men desire the terms to be inclusive. They want individualism with collectivism, freedom with authority.

And yet it must be confessed that the omens are not propitious. We have had good cause to know that in extending the authority of the State it is not easy to preserve the liberty of the individual. The rise of Communism, Fascism, and Nazism in Europe was not comforting for those who wished to see the common man enjoy his rights and privileges. Even in our own country the extension of the powers of the State has been at the expense of the individual. John Knox's 'monstrous regiment' is a term one might use of the ubiquitous Civil Service.

The same process is at work in industry. The rise from master and man to the combine, the monopoly, and so to control, direct or indirect, of the State, has altered the whole position of the workman. The old craftsman is in danger of becoming a memory. The process of mass production makes men machine-minders. The man performing his own small operation as he stands in his particular place by the endlessly moving conveyor belt has no opportunity of knowing the worth and dignity of labour. He often does not know the various processes, apart from his own, by which the finished article is made. Like the genie in 'Aladdin', he is the slave of the lamp. He is apt to feel that he is a mere cog in a vast impersonal machine with none to know him and none to care.

Tom, Dick, and Harry want the fullest opportunity to lead the good life, but they are oppressed with fear and doubt. They have excellent reason to be. The rights of natural man are a fiction. The political philosophers of the eighteenth century elaborated the theory that man had certain elementary rights which he did not surrender but rather had guaranteed to him when he contracted himself out of society into the State. Locke allowed, under certain extreme conditions, the right of revolt against the State if these rights were denied. But Rousseau went farther. He drew the conventional eighteenth-century picture of man as leading at first an innocent noble simple life and then he represented the State, not as preserving man's original freedom, but taking it away. 'Man was born free, but is everywhere in chains.' The right and even the duty of rebellion was made obvious. It is a short step from *Le Contrat Social* to the cry of 'Liberty! Equality! Fraternity!' At the same time as the Paris mobs were asserting their rights, Godwin and Paine were teaching in England the sacrosanctity of these same rights. And so the whole edifice of nineteenth-century liberalism was built upon a doubtful theory in political philosophy. It was inevitable that when storms came the building should totter and fall. It is possible to note the change in thought even in the later works of Herbert Spencer and John Stuart Mill. In the works of Mazzini the movement away from the doctrine of rights is clearly apparent. An even stronger trumpet blast was sounded in the writings of Marx and Engels. When T. H. Green delivered his lectures on the principles of political obligation, the old individualism had finally given place to collectivism in political thinking.

Just as a man cannot live except in community, so an individual has no rights apart from his rights as a member of a community. It was realized that as man cannot be conceived living his life apart from the State, so it is inconceivable that he has rights over against the State. This does not mean that he must blindly accept the dictates of the State, but only that when he stands out against the command of the State he does it not in his own interest but in what he thinks is the common interest. Thus when a man states his conscientious objection to war he does it in obedience to a higher loyalty which he believes to be ultimately for the general good.

But if he has no justifiable rights in the modern world as an isolated individual, is a man's position much more secure as a member of the State? Is John Citizen so much better off? The record of this century is that collectivism can easily slide into State tyranny. The individual member of the State finds to his dismay that he is only expected to obey. Over large tracts of Europe liberalism and democracy are spurned and men accept the complete authority of the State. 'The greater the power the more dangerous the abuse', said Edmund Burke, and the modern State increasingly asks for the worship once accorded to God. For it has in part assumed the attributes of God. It is omniscient, omnipresent, and omnipotent. The prospect is dark indeed.

Man has no rights in himself either as an individual or as a member of a State. For if you regard man apart from God he is only a higher form of anthropoid ape thrown up by chance on the shores of time and doomed to perish everlastingly. Like other animals he must struggle and fight and die. Since therefore the universe is entirely neutral, the question of morality does not arise. You need not have the slightest compunction in

man to make the world safe for democracy. But the democracy that survived the war had lost much of its shining lustre. On the Continent it was openly derided and trampled under-foot. But even in this country it was subject to cold criticism. I well remember in the years following the war, Studdert Kennedy, better known as 'Woodbine Willie', addressing a meeting of undergraduates in the Guildhall, Cambridge. He said a friend of his who was a psycho-analyst had tried on him the practice of Word-association. He shouted a word and Kennedy had to reply at once with the first word that occurred to him. By and by he shouted, 'Democracy', and Studdert Kennedy replied, 'Despair'. That attitude was general. People realized that Democratic government of itself was not sufficient. If people were too lazy or careless to use their votes, or if in the use of their votes they were too easily subject to mass suggestion, democracy would not function properly. Vision and character were needed if the machinery of government was ever to run smoothly and efficiently.

The same truth was realized in the case of trade and industry. After the war in which the loser was to pay all our debts, and make good all our losses, and we were all going to be prosperous, we found economics did not work so simply as that. Norman Angell and J. Maynard Keynes were surprisingly right. We had to accustom ourselves to a situation in which, whilst food was being destroyed, multitudes were hungry to the point of starvation. There was potential plenty, but untold numbers of men throughout the world were eating out their hearts in idleness. In such a situation that but for its stark tragedy would have been Gilbertian, men recognized that the mere fact of trade and industry was not sufficient to herald an era of prosperity. Behind economics must be vision and character.

But the failure of Education, Science, Democracy, and Economics, to deliver the goods, was ultimately the failure of man. The truth could not be hidden. Men were not big enough for their task. This realization brought a condition of despair. From an optimistic humanism men swiftly fell into a chill pessimism in which they were haunted by their own insufficiency. The more lighthearted were able to shrug their shoulders and argue that since nothing could be done, why worry about anything? They eagerly listened to the teaching of a sex mysticism which was being propounded by Aldous Huxley and D. H.

Lawrence in the nineteen-twenties. It was in these years that London had its 'bright young things'. Now alas! they are neither very bright nor very young. The lightest of farces and musical comedies had abnormally long runs on the stage in this same decade. The outstanding literary figure of the twenties was James Joyce, and his most famous book, *Ulysses* (1922), is a sign and symbol of his times. Here was a great creative artist who had cut himself adrift from his old moorings and who had no compass to guide him in his voyaging. His modern Ulysses, Leopold Bloom, only wanders from domesticity for a single day, but his adventures are dictated by his own wants and appetites. It is a picture thrown on an immense canvas of man's futility, and his inadequacy to meet the challenge of great events.

But as the sky grew darker the prevailing mood became more sombre. The mirth of the frivolous became 'the crackling of thorns under a pot'. It was now that the influence of T. S. Eliot became so generally felt. His *Waste Land* (1922) appeared in the same year as *Ulysses*; here, however, was no hedonism but only despair. *The Hollow Men* (1925) was another experiment in the same manner. His masochistic readers delighted in his flagellation. They believed him to be right in describing us as hollow men and stuffed men leaning together. And how grimly true his conclusion seemed to be:

> *This is the way the world ends;*
> *Not with a bang but a whimper.*

T. S. Eliot passed from nihilism to religious conviction in *Ash Wednesday* (1930), and in all his later work, but it was this earlier Eliot who influenced profoundly the brilliant young poets writing in the thirties—W. H. Auden, Stephen Spender, Louis Macneice, Dylan Thomas, and Cecil Day Lewis. This decade was sterner than the last, and whilst the poets had no illusions about man they were not sterile in their despair. Increasingly they looked to the left in their demand for social change and for some bulwark against the rising tide of Nazism and Fascism.

Each of them in his own way had stressed the abyss in the human soul. Amongst contemporary thinkers it was Berdyaev who pictured most vividly the heaven and hell in every man.

Meanwhile those who were interested in literature and philosophy were turning with fresh eyes to Pascal, Kierkegaard, and Dostoevski.

But for the average student interested in religious thought the greatest name was unquestionably Karl Barth. Jacques Maritain has said that Barthianism was a complete reversal of humanism, for it 'annihilated man before God'. And in Barth's writings the pendulum had swung to its opposite extreme. Whereas man has been regarded as naturally good, now he was regarded as naturally bad. In his fidelity to Calvin, Barth seemed to revive the teaching of man's total depravity. But if man is wholly corrupt he is incapable of any goodness. Barth in avoiding Scylla had foundered on Charybdis. And yet this description of man is significant, for the enormous influence of Barth showed how profoundly his despair of man accorded with prevailing opinion. This view of human nature, though in a much modified and more realistic way, was accepted by the great American theologian Reinhold Niebuhr. In theological circles a little jest became widely known:

Thou shalt love thy Barth with all thy heart
And thy Niebuhr as thyself.

But even more symptomatic of contemporary thought was the reverence paid to Sigmund Freud by all those interested in psychology. His theory of the unconscious, whilst very distressing to those who still believed in the greatness of man, was accepted as a true account of the tangled undergrowth of human nature. When he died, *The Times*, in an obituary notice, described his teaching as a brilliant commentary on the doctrine of original sin. And so by strange paradox the agnostic Freud found himself in company with Paul, Augustine, Luther, and Wesley.

It was at this time that (perhaps because of Paul Tillich's influence) the word 'demonic' was freely used to describe those dark forces in the world that opposed the truth. There were some, notably Karl Heim, who went farther and did not hesitate to speak of the existence of a personal Devil.

In truth there was much in the third decade of the century to confirm any thinker in his despair of man's inability to save himself. In this period there was the great economic collapse in which untold numbers went bankrupt and the figures of unemployed soared to astronomical heights. It was a period of naked aggression, marked by such names as Manchukuo, Abyssinia, China, Spain, Czechoslovakia, and which moved inevitably to the nemesis of September 1939. These were the days when men learnt with horror of the recrudescence of racial animosity, the persecution of the Jews, the bullying of weaker nations, the concentration camps and the dread Gestapo. Beneath the thin veneer of civilization the wild and primitive instincts of the jungle were plain for all to see. War brought its fresh horrors, but it could not add any new facts. It could only deepen even more the sense of impotence and despair. Within a generation the world was again the scene of bloody conflict and the babies of the first world war were being sent to fight in the second. Whilst the war continued the need for action enabled men to trample down their despair. Then came the tumult and the shouting. The bonfires were lit and the flags hung out. But the biggest bonfire sinks to ashes and the bravest flag becomes bedraggled. Since V.E. and V.J. days we have had leisure to enjoy the fruits of victory, and in the prevailing fear and insecurity, nothing can hide from us a knowledge of our own weakness. Once more we are face to face with our own despair.

In such a situation there are certain voices which speak to us more loudly than the rest. A writer in the *Spectator* spoke recently of the religion of 'futilitarianism'. It is born of a sense of disillusionment and despair, and because it can discern no pattern and no purpose in life it cries out, 'Ah, what's the use?' Behind the alarming figures of expenditure in drink and gambling, behind the disturbing rise in divorce cases, there is this malaise of spirit. Because so many have lost God and are without hope, they take the line of least resistance and fall in with majority opinion. Since there is none to care, each man is answerable to himself alone. In such a situation let a man grab what satisfaction he can. When a man attacks contemporary social evils he must address himself to this spiritual exhaustion. To denounce evils of today is not enough. One must understand the underlying causes.

The vogue of this modern cult must not be underestimated. In its philosophic form on the continent of Europe it is called existentialism (from a phrase of Kierkegaard), and its call on the individual is to seek his own salvation by action rather than thought in a situation which is tragic and grotesque. In the work of Jean Paul Sartre it is a call to freedom by one's own efforts or by an heroic resignation. It is wholly agnostic, and even in its most eloquent expression has no lifebelt to fling to a drowning man. Despite the influence of Kierkegaard the existentialists come to a wholly different conclusion from him. He said:

'Relate thyself relatively to the relative and absolutely to the absolute.' They say in effect: 'Relate thyself absolutely to the relative', and that is indeed a counsel of despair.

There are two other solutions offered. We are asked to be saved by science or to be saved by politics. This is still the day of the scientist. His achievements have been so formidable that though they have a boomerang action, his prestige is still un-dimmed. One of Napoleon's soldiers is reported to have said when Napoleon came back from Elba: 'Shall not I whose nose was frozen for him at Moscow fight for him again?' And many who are staggered at the efficiency of the destructive weapons of science in warfare are persuaded similarly to give their unthinking support to scientific humanism. The utopian schemes of H. G. Wells have always had a large and interested public, and now there are so many ready to accept the scientific attitude of C. H. Waddington, the religion of Julian Huxley, and to walk with followers of the late Sir James Jeans along the milky way. They will not realize from H. G. Wells's later writings that there is no pessimism so unrelieved as that of the optimist gone sour.

Truth does not go by suffrage, and despite the vast number who look to the scientist for deliverance, our salvation will not come that way. The reason is obvious. The scientist can measure, describe and analyse, but when he attempts to interpret, he passes out of the domain of science into philosophy. For science is concerned with the how and not with the why of things. In consequence the scientist speaks as a private individual when he assumes the role of a prophet. He has just as much authority and no more than any other man who speaks outside his own province. Despite Plato, the world has never found its philo-sopher kings though they have been sought with tears. And scientists with all their skill, integrity, and single-mindedness are not qualified for that high office.

But supposing for one mad moment that they had the ultimate wisdom, and supposing that their new world was the best possible world for mortals to live in, how do they propose to bring us out of the wilderness into that Canaan of their dreams? They have perforce to rely on the fine white light of reason. As they them-selves are guided by it, so they expect others will follow the same leading. But this is surely to be deficient both in psychology and in a sense of history. Even if the Latin tag, 'I approve the better, I follow the worse', be forgotten, even if Augustine be put on one side, surely Freud has a pertinent word to say to those who trust that men will be sweetly reasonable. Reason can so often be at the mercy of those deep instinctive urges whose seat is in the unconscious mind.

And haven't these same scientists learnt anything from history? Have not the events of the last thirty years taught them any lesson? We have witnessed a flight from reason. We have recoiled in horror from those blind irrational forces which have threatened to destroy us all. Pascal said that if man was a reed he was a thinking reed, but we have lived in a world in which one of the most prominent leaders of Germany wanted to reach for a gun at the sound of the word culture. All the fruits of reason— tolerance, sympathy, and understanding—have been flouted and derided. The virtues of the barbarian have been again extolled; irrational outworn theories of race, blood, and soil, have again been revived. In the early days of the French Revolution a beautiful courtesan was carried through the streets of Paris as the Goddess of Reason and there were multitudes to do her honour. It is true, alas! that within a short time she was forgotten and men were swept along by wilder passions. But in our time the poor Goddess has in many countries not even been paid the tribute of lip service. Even those most attached to her service have found themselves strangely impotent. The racing millstream is heedless of the scandalized looks of polite bystanders. Surely it has been apparent to all that man is not swayed by pure reason nor guided by it. The scientist overlooks that fatal self-contradiction in man through which he can destroy both his works and himself.

There is another way of salvation offered to man in his despair. It is the way of the politician. Accept a particular programme and you will achieve the new order. There are many so impressed by the stupendous achievements of Soviet Russia both in peace and war that they believe that some such scheme of state socialism, consonant with our own history and genius, would solve our problems and ensure our happy future.

But would the Utopia of the politician or social reformer be any more comfortable to live in than that of the scientist? If you are able to give a man efficient public services, if he can have his little house and garden in the suburban housing estate, have you given him all he needs? Feed a lap dog, keep him warm, watch his health, and you have given him all he needs. But can an immortal soul be treated in that same way? If eternity has been set in his heart can he ever be wholly satisfied by placing his treasure where moth and rust corrupt, and where thieves can break through and steal.

But even supposing that the politician—economist—social reformer—can provide satisfaction for all man's physical, mental, and spiritual needs, is not his dilemma still that of the scientist? How is he going to get us in through the golden gates? How can he contend with the selfishness, greed, envy, and suspicion which is in the heart of man? How can he overcome his inertia? How will he free him from that downward pull which has brought man to despair of himself? He has no better hopes than the scientist and no better prospects. They may give us an idea of where to go. They may even propose a method of getting there, but they cannot show us how to do it. They cannot deliver men because they have no means of coping with the depths of human nature.

In the divine strategy, this is the day of opportunity. For when a man comes to an end of himself he can make a beginning with God. When he despairs of himself, he can look up, for his deliverance draws near. It was when men were most assured and confident that our Lord knew them to be in the greatest danger. His woes were directed against the rich and satisfied. His beatitudes were for those who had nothing and therefore were able to possess all. If a man is self-sufficient, God can do nothing for him, because the man does not need him. But if a man despairs of himself he has but to take one step more. He must believe. The word is always repent and believe. Turn from yourself that you may turn to God. It is when we are naked that we are prepared to turn to Him for dress; when we are helpless we look to Him for grace, and only when we are foul do we fly to the fountain. If modern man in his despair knows himself to be lost, he is in an excellent situation, for it was precisely the lost whom Jesus came to seek and to save.

It is only in Christian Theology that the dualism of man's nature is frankly and fully faced, and a decisive way of deliverance shown. The doctrine of original sin does justice both to the divine origin of man and to his subsequent fall. God breathed into man and he became a living soul. The spirit of man, said the Psalmist, is the candle of the Lord. The ordinary man peers through the giant telescope at worlds upon worlds in endless space. He knows from Jeans that nine wasps spread between England and Siberia would occupy more space than those stars in the silent immensities, and his heart fails him. Man is puny, said Pascal, and knows that he is puny. The universe is great and knows not that it is great, and therefore man is greater than the universe. The Christian holds in contempt the beslavering of men with a slick writer's spittle. He knows that man was made in God's image and that God looks and loves His image there. He may stare moodily over a pigsty but he was meant for the Father's love. God meant him to sit in heavenly places. There is no room here for ultimate pessimism. Man's wildest hopes for himself are but a faint imperfect shadow of God's intention. And yet left to himself he cannot save himself. In his unaided strength, there is no deliverance.

He is made in the image of God, but that image is defaced. Made by God, and made for God, he is yet separated from God. Because of his disobedience he who was meant to be theocentric has become egocentric and is therefore at cross purposes with himself. Made for heaven, he yet feels the gravitational tug of earth. With his nature corrupted and his will biased, he cannot free himself from his own chains. And so he cries out in his despair that the evil he would not, that he does, and the good he ought to do, he does not. By all means let a man pull down a well-thumbed volume from his library shelves, or pull his chair closer to the fire as he converses with a friend. Let him listen to a Beethoven symphony or throw himself on the grassy hillside as he watches puffs of white clouds form only to dissolve again. Every aid to man's culture of spirit is needed, every sound, every colour, every inward whisper. But ransack civilization, turn out her every treasure. There will be much to make a beggar rich. But there will not be pardon, nor cleansing, nor renewal. The world and the mind of man have their own essential treasures, but they cannot speak the delivering word to an imprisoned spirit which lies 'fast bound in sin and nature's night'.

Man cannot save himself because he is the subject of an eternal tug of war, nor can he be saved by any of his fellows for they are infected by the same malady. No scientific plan, nor social order, nor political society, can wholly meet his need, for however adequate they might be, he could by his own sinful folly wreck them all. The man with a slum mentality would change even a palace into a slum. And natural man has shown how he can

make even heaven into hell. We live today in a fair world that
has become a bloody shambles.

His case is so desperate that it demands nothing less than the
desperate remedy of the Cross. If man is the sinner that all
history has shown him to be, then he can only be saved by grace.
The intervention of God in Jesus Christ is the one true answer
to our need. By His love for the unlovely we are not only freed
from the guilt of sin but from its power. He alone can save us
and since he is willing to save us, nothing can prevent our
salvation but ourselves.

There is something which is at once exhilarating and satisfying in this Christian message for man and society. The Church
which proclaims this message is neither optimistic nor pessimistic
about man. It knows that whilst all men are sinners and therefore capable of infinite mischief, all men have immortal longings
and are therefore capable of infinite goodness. Since men are
the children of God they will inevitably suffer pain and frustra-
tion apart from Him. But if they respond to His love and live
in His Society they will fulfil their destiny. It is axiomatic that
if we live for ourselves we shall die, but it is just as true that if
we live by ourselves we shall likewise perish. It is only when we
live with God that we are able to live with each other, and with
ourselves. So that to live at all we needs must live with God.
This is the condition of entrance into the Kingdom and this is
the true meaning of history. The ages do not record the grotesque
convolutions of unhappy creatures in an eerie dance of death,
but they witness to the good pleasure of God in giving us the
Kingdom.

In the coming of that Kingdom all can take their part. There
is the task of removing hindrances to God's entrance into human
hearts. Private sins and social habits which cloud the vision,
blunt spiritual sensibilities, deflect a man from his true direction,
are obviously to be condemned. When people attack those social
habits which hinder the living of the good life it is because such
practices kill joy and spoil sport. In every age God needs workmen who will strive to remove those barriers which prevent men
from possessing their lawful possession. When Henry Burton in
a well-known hymn said,

He is breaking down the barriers, He is casting up the way,[a]

a *Methodist Hymn-book*, No. 256 (1933).

he rightly went on to say it is we who help Him in that task:

His angels here are human, not the shining hosts above.[a]

But if barriers are to be broken, right conditions must be created for God to take His power and reign. No hard and fast distinction can be drawn between those who serve God's increasing purpose and those who do not. Every worker whose task is useful and who performs it faithfully is a worker for the Kingdom.

Every task, however simple, sets the soul that does it free;
Every deed of love and mercy done to man, is done to Me.
Nevermore thou needest seek Me; I am with thee everywhere;
Raise the stone, and thou shalt find Me; cleave the wood and I am there.[b]

It is not only memorials and public buildings which can be dedicated to the glory of God. When parents seek their children's good, when the workman sees beyond his pay packet and his private interests, when the industrialist is concerned with ultimates and not alone with immediates; when in Edmund Burke's phrase, statesmen are 'men of light and leading', the greater glory of God is served.

And yet when all this is done the purpose of God is not fully consummated. It is clearly God's will that hindrances be removed and right conditions created, but only as means to a larger end. The man living at last in his dream house, and possessed of modern gadgets, has not thereby been delivered from greed and selfishness, nor miraculously endowed with virtues not known before. Pardon and peace and renewal are not to be purchased by man. They are the gift of God.

That is why all the many builders of God, the conscious and the unconscious instruments of His purpose, depend for the consummation of their labours upon the faithfulness of the Church. There can be no Kingdom without a King. All other work is completed by God's work within the heart. To the Church is committed this proclamation of man's dependence on God. Only in that obedience to God can selfishness be cast out, and a man be made afresh. Not man alone, nor God alone, but God and man together can bring us to a world in which the little child can be set in the midst unharmed and unafraid.

Into the fellowship of this one Church we invite the children of men. All may come, for all are needed. And within that

a Methodist Hymn-book, No. 256 (1933).   *b* ibid., No. 601.

faithful company, each, instructed by the Holy Spirit, may apply himself to his own task. The clerk, the teacher, the research student, the miner and the housewife can make their jobs a vehicle of God's grace. Through their life and witness the word of reconciliation can be proclaimed. The page boy may be an ambassador, for God supplies credentials to all who apply, and sends His envoys where He will.

The Church in the Middle Ages said that salvation could only be found in the fellowship of His Church. The Reformers in their insistence on salvation by faith, said that salvation must be individually appropriated. God's word for our day is that whilst salvation is within the fellowship and must be individually received, the one Church is the one instrument bringing men into the one Kingdom. It receives and crowns the work of good men everywhere. Each member within the Church doing what he honestly feels to be within the interests of the Kingdom is part of that militant fellowship against which the gates of Hell shall not prevail. The message for the Church in the twentieth century lies in this fresh understanding and exploration of the Reformation emphasis on the priesthood of all believers.

Inside the Church as well as outside the Church there is the continual work of helping to remove hindrances and create the right conditions of life, but to the Church alone is given a word which none other can utter. Outside the fellowship of the Church there can be no evangelical task: no call to repent and believe, to see and to serve. But this call literally is the crux of the matter. The offer of grace is an offer of life. A Church commissioned to proclaim this Gospel has the keys of the Kingdom. And having the keys of the Kingdom it has the keys of the future.

Printed in Great Britain by
The Camelot Press Ltd., London and Southampton